Copyright © 2019 Roger Morgan-Grenville
Illustrations © 2019 Oliver Preston

First published in the UK in 2019
by Quiller, an imprint of Quiller Publishing Ltd

British Library Cataloguing-in-Publication Data
A catalogue record for this book is available from
the British Library

ISBN 978 1 84689 292 9

Printed in the Czech Republic

Whilst every effort has been made to obtain permission from copyright
holders for all material used in this book, the publishers will be pleased to
hear from anyone who has not been appropriately acknowledged, and to
make the correction in future reprints.

Quiller

An imprint of Quiller Publishing Ltd
Wykey House, Wykey, Shrewsbury SY4 1JA
Tel: 01939 261616
Email: info@quillerbooks.com
Website: www.quillerpublishing.com

Dedicated to the Tree Hugger, without whose
strange telephone call back in July 1986,
I would most likely never have played cricket
again. And without whose early enthusiasm,
the White Hunter Cricket Club would certainly
never have happened.

Contents

Foreword

HAROLD Pinter once said, 'I tend to think that cricket is the greatest thing that God ever created on earth – certainly better than sex,' a sentiment with which two of the heroes of this book (no spoilers) demonstrably agree. But it's not the elite-level cricket that forms the staple diet of my day job as a radio commentator to which they refer. It's not marvelling at Ben Stokes cracking 258 at Cape Town, or purring as Virat Kohli creams effortless cover drives off 90-miles-per-hour Australian bowlers. It's not passive. It's active.

Broadcasters and writers tend to fixate exclusively on cricket in England through the prism of the professional game, in which around five hundred men and women ply their trade. Occasionally there is concern expressed about decreasing participation in the amateur game, but the solutions seldom involve existing cricket players and fans; instead we are told by administrators that initiatives must appeal to people who currently don't like cricket. People who think that rather than being better than sex, it might, at a pinch, be better than a poke in the eye with a sharp stick.

In a former life, I was captain of an amateur team for twenty years. It was the hardest and most rewarding thing I've ever done. Maintaining equanimity in the face of a tornado of Friday night and Saturday morning cry-offs is the least of it. Among many other things, you must be an impresario, counsellor, caterer and event organiser. The least of your jobs is actually to be a cricketer.

This book is for all those admirable and patient souls who remain calm when their opening bowler tells them on Saturday morning that his hand is stuck in the car door and he won't be able to make it. For the captain who must sound delighted when his leading batsman tells him in February that his wife is expecting a baby in May, so he won't be around for the cricket season. For the captain who must mask his joy at the unexpected return of his star all-rounder, who has been missing for three years but is now back after the acrimonious breakdown of his marriage. But it's also about the 750,000 dedicated amateurs that play the game and the millions more who used to play it, but simply can't anymore. The men and women who believe that this will be the week they score that hundred, or perfect that unplayable doosra. It's for people who, after a week of under-appreciation and endless demands from their (probably cricket-averse) bosses, whether in an office or factory, shop or building site, have the sanctuary of cricket where the only demands are the ones they place on themselves. Demands for a fifty, a couple of wickets, or the occasional spectacular catch. Demands that are almost always thwarted by their own and their teammates enduring shortcomings. But come what may, they'll get to blame the umpires for being sawn off just as they were getting their eye in, and take the piss out of the skipper for being too old and slow to saunter in the four yards required to take the bloody catch. They will stagger home with a hot, tanned face, a grazed knee from their sliding stop, and a comforting stiffness of the muscles that makes no sense, because they haven't really done anything today. At the end of the season, they've got a mountain of those memories. They've got that fifty. They've got that perfectly timed lofted thwack over mid-off for their only six. They've got an instinctive one-handed wonder catch. They've got the odd wicket as well. They've got the occasional victory. But most importantly, they've got their friendships.

This book is for the people that make cricket both possible and the most magical game on earth, and yes, very possibly better than sex.

Dan Norcross

Introduction

THREE-QUARTERS of a million people play cricket in Britain in thousands of different clubs. This is a story of one of those clubs, in only one season.

Any sport club that survives more than a handful of years will have something more than the sport itself that binds it together, something else that defines it. It might be excellence, region, occupation, disability or even religion: once we had a match 'cancelled through the effects of Ramadan'. Most often, though, it is simply plain friendship. It is the excuse for people to enjoy the company of others through the prism of a shared enthusiasm. We all think our club is special and the irony is, we are all right. When a club stops being special to its members, it quickly folds. So, by a process of logic, these are stories of friendships long before they are stories of cricket.

The White Hunter Cricket Club was born on 19 July 1986. We formed up because a team called the Rhinos had asked whether anyone in the Winchester area wanted a match, and two or three of us rather fancied the idea. We came together for just that one match and called ourselves the White Hunters, because we had the childish notion that the name would irritate a team called the Rhinos, which it didn't; they thought it was rather charming. We went on to lose, and only four of us turned out again when the match was reprised the following year.

We lost again, but something about it all appealed to a small group of us, and we set up six fixtures for the following year, then eight, then ten, and so on. After that it was a logo, and the club sweaters and caps that inevitably followed. We ventured out of Hampshire and in 1990, did our first 'overseas' tour. It was a long weekend in Yorkshire and, in those pre-internet days, we were unable to discover before it was too late that our Sunday opposition were actually second in the Tetleys Yorkshire League and had members who could bowl at eighty miles per hour. Rain helped us to scrape a draw, and we felt invincible.

France followed a while later, where our notion that we were going to meet incompetent players called Guillaume, with bunches of onions strung across their bike frames, evaporated in the cruelty of an utter drubbing at the hands of expat Australian and Caribbean cricketers, on a field by the bend in the Loire River at Saumur.

Over the next thirty-three seasons, we have played exactly 100 oppositions, on eighty-five grounds, in 386 separate games, and with the services of 342 players. We have won 135 of those games, lost 189, drawn 53, tied seven, and death has stopped one. And yes, we are aware that the maths doesn't work. Somewhere out there is a match that none of us have the faintest recollection of being involved in, and yet we know that we played it.

During those years we grew from being young men, possibly with girlfriends, to being married, and then having young children, then getting those teenage children to play. My oldest son is now only three years younger than I was when we set up the club. Cricket has an odd habit of being dynastic, so this story is about time as well, time as measured equally in drop scones and dropped catches, and time as a commodity that goes only one way. As much as anything, the story of the club is also the story of defiance: of age, injury and, often enough, common sense.

When you are not very good at something – as I am, and we are at cricket – people mistakenly assume that we are content with this, that we are happy to be the joker out there. They could not be more wrong. Everyone who goes out there for those seventy sunlit weekend overs, does so in the shadow of a reckless dream that this might be their day, and a determination to amount to more than the sum of their parts.

Most of the time, it doesn't happen, but just occasionally, often enough to make us react to the bugle call of the following season, some tiny act of near brilliance happens to us, or gets associated with us, that brings us a yard or two closer to our heaven. It is what makes us go on, and the reason why we paint the corners of our lives with cricket.

Friendship, dynasty, defiance and hope. That is why we do it. And those teas.

1 The Librarians

September

ONLY one of them wasn't a librarian, and even he was a library assistant.

The sole game plan we had for our fixture against the Bodleian Librarians was for the entire team to shout '*Shhhhh!*'very loudly at the moment of their first appeal, and then to congratulate ourselves for our spectacular wit, even if it turned out they didn't share the joke. It wasn't much of a plan, to be sure, but we were sustained and encouraged by the fact that this was one more than we normally managed.

Plans and the White Hunter Cricket Club are like ships

passing at a distance on a foggy night. We normally make plans only in reaction to the unexpected things that happen along the way, such as someone forgetting to switch on the urn for tea, or a car alarm going off because a stray sheep was rubbing its backside against the vehicle concerned. In those kinds of situations, we are masters of strategy; anything to do with cricket is far more complicated, and we tend to avoid interfering with it.

By tradition, I like to stand at mid on when I captain a team, and it was from there that I scanned the players around me, as the Graduate prepared to bowl the opening ball of the 35-over-a-side game, the last of our English season. We had never played this side before, so the air was pregnant with possibilities, ranging from their being very much better than us, to their being even worse than us, with both of us being roughly the same somewhere in the middle.

The jury was still out, but we could already tell from the way that the opener had walked out from the pavilion, acknowledged our polite applause, and then readied himself for the first over, that he had the air of a seasoned cricketer. He did that kind of stuff you do when you're quite good, like swinging his bat around his shoulder in a lethal arc, and executing complex groundworks in the marking out of his crease. I'd been working hard on that aspect of my game during the past season, and so understood it well.

The Graduate, who doubled as my twenty-three-year-old son, Tom, was excited about this fixture, as the opposition came from the city in which he had so recently been a student. The city was Oxford and, whilst the librarians came from the distinguished end of town serving the ancient university that gave us M.J.K. Smith, C.B. Fry and Imran Khan, the Graduate had been at the bit in the north end of town that used to be a polytechnic, but now calls itself Brookes, and therefore cheerfully charges its students the same fees as its more illustrious neighbour.

He hadn't been remotely interested in cricket until he was about sixteen, but since then he had worked hard on his game, and these days no one on earth could theorise more about it than him: bat grips, seam positions and fielding strategies all queued up to be commented on. It didn't matter whether you were Joe Bloggs or Virat Kohli, the Graduate would have advice for you as skipper, whether you had asked for it or not. Particularly if you hadn't. And he would have theories as to why things were happening the way they were.

Under the Dewey Decimal System of book classification – as we are temporarily in the company of librarians – you might dual file him under 822 (English Drama and Suspense) and 123 (Indeterminism), on the basis that his cricketing outcomes are related more to chance than anything else.

'Play!' said the genial umpire, and a pause ensued, during which a small issue manifested itself: we didn't have a ball. Whilst one was being shipped out to the middle, the Graduate told me that he had a particular plan for the first ball, which he then duly bowled off a shortened run-up. It turned out that the batsman had a particular plan for it as well, which was to deposit it into an adjacent allotment.

Fine leg, in the form of the Breeder (636 Animal Husbandry), trotted off to retrieve it. Despite being our fastest and most reliable bowler, a trot was as quick as he ever got, and he tended only to go that fast in emergencies. Having recovered the ball, he walked back and lobbed it by relay via square leg and back to the bowler. I knew that the Breeder had two things on his mind at that moment – the livestock that he was taking to the Usk Agricultural Show the following morning, and the fact that he was bowling the second over.

'Bad luck, Tom,' he said, as if the batsman had got away with a ridiculously lucky shot, rather than dispatched a rank long hop.

And that is the essential problem with the Breeder, he can't help himself being polite and positive. Even when he appeals for an lbw or a catch behind, he does so in quiet tones to the umpire, as if picking up on a previous philosophical conversation, and giving a decision in his favour might be only one of the things occupying his busy mind.

The Graduate went back to the mark of his longer run-up and bowled a straight and respectable ball on the off stump, which the batsman prodded out in the direction of the Tree Hugger at short mid off.

The dictionary tells us that dreams are 'a succession of images occurring involuntarily', which rather neatly describes the Tree Hugger's bowling, so we shall allocate him 135 (Dreams and Mysteries) in our club library. He and I were jointly responsible for setting up this club, and we have spent exactly a third of a century organising, chasing, cajoling, comforting, persuading, pleading, scolding, lying and apologising on its behalf ever since.

That our relationship has survived the slings and arrows of outrageous fortune over the years that the club has been going is almost entirely down to our practice of alternating captaining duties, and of spending inordinate numbers of winter evenings in the Harrow Inn at Steep wishing we were better cricketers. We are the glue that holds the club together, in the sense that glue is the by-product of the meat-rendering business, and all that is left once the animals have gone.

His is the pedantic yin to my attention-deficit yang, a bachelor, the accumulator of statistics and the monitor of the club's behaviour. He runs a hedging business, and had once informed us, unwisely in strict confidence, that he had gone on a dating site with the alias 'Tree Hugger', and he has never quite shaken off the name.

He lobbed the ball back to the Graduate, who then repeated

the same delivery, only this time on the leg stump. The batsman pushed it respectfully square in the direction of the Gun Runner, who collected it and shouted 'Shabash!' at the bowler.

No one really knew what the Gun Runner did, but his air of prosperous bonhomie and the fact that he lived in a large and exquisite house in the centre of a very desirable village suggested that it was not without its rewards. And whatever it was, it seemed to entail many short-notice visits to parts of the world that weren't only not at peace, but normally involved in some form of ill-suppressed conflict.

Gingerly, when he got back from one of these trips, we would ask him 'how it had all gone', and he would respond with a twinkle that he really couldn't grumble, and then regale us with unlikely tales of gunfights at dawn on the edge of North African goldfields, and of seedy evenings spent in downtown Mogadishu in the company of men called Abdul, who knew rather too much about piracy for comfort. It all made our parochial existences in the valleys of West Sussex and East Hampshire seem tedious in the extreme.

Once, when he and I were being bombarded with short bowling by a team of Afghan refugees from a camp near Bergerac, he had listened to about twenty minutes of excited inter-team chatter before announcing in flawless Pashtun that, if they really wanted to knock his block off as they said they did, they would have to bowl both a good deal straighter, and faster, than they were currently. The effect on them was electric, and when the match was over, it was clear that he had made new friends for life. (753 Symbolism, Allegory, Myth and Legend).

The Gun Runner threw the ball back at the Graduate, who proceeded to bowl his fourth ball. For once, whatever the theory was, it came off. The ball swung in the air and then cut back off the seam, taking a thin edge on its way through to the Human

Sieve (127 The Unconscious and the Subconscious) behind the stumps. Someone usefully shouted, 'Catch it!' and, to be fair, that thought probably presented itself to the Sieve among various others at some stage in the half second or two that it took the ball to get to him.

But then different counsels prevailed and, in snatching at it with the tip of his gloved right finger, he sent the ball scudding along the ground to third man. Few fielders, and almost no keepers, have the fundamental porosity of the Human Sieve; that unique ability to wave a ball through towards its ultimate destiny on the boundary rope. However, he seems condemned forever to be the club's first-choice wicket-keeper. He doesn't know why, and neither do we. We just turn up at a ground and he puts the pads on.

'Ooops. Sorry, Tom,' said the Sieve.

'Oh, bad luck!' said the Breeder.

The Graduate looked to the heavens, and thought better of the acidic something he was about to say.

The run conceded had brought the other opener to face his first ball, and he duly took his guard. The Graduate theatrically asked square leg to go deep, and the batsman, equally theatrically, practised a hook shot, to make the point that he didn't really care where the fielders were, or what the potential trap was, and he would play whatever shot he would play. With the batsman not caring, and the bowler not really knowing what the next delivery was, it satisfied everyone that it ended up as a full ball on middle and off, which was duly patted back to the bowler.

'Shabash!' said the Gun Runner.

'Well done!' said the Breeder.

'Join the dots,' said the Sieve, oblivious to the fact that the over had gone for seven runs already, and there weren't really any dots to join.

The sixth ball, when it came, was by far the worst of the over. It was a long hop, two foot outside the off stump. If it could speak, it would have been saying provocatively, 'Hit me! Hit me!' As it was, the ball was an unspoken invitation that the batsman couldn't ignore. He pivoted back onto his right leg, much like Gordon Greenidge used to do in that prolific West Indian summer of 1976, and duly cracked the ball off the bottom edge of his bat straight down onto his off stump. Seven for one after one over, which, in our world, counts as a cracking start.

Once the Graduate had accepted the plaudits of his teammates, he caught my eye and winked at me, in a manner that meant to say: 'I told you I had a plan.'

IT is for days such as these that we live our summer lives.

We wake up on the previous Monday morning and know instinctively that the coming week won't be all that bad, because there is a cricket match at the end of it. And one in a pretty village against a new opposition, which makes it all the better. From then on, we think about it more than is healthy for us.

We drop off to sleep on Tuesday night with the dream of our left foot taking a step forward towards the pitch of the ball, to caress it through the packed offside field to the cover boundary. The commentators call this 'threading the needle'; the left side of our brains call it 'utter fiction'.

We check our emails on Friday morning to make sure that no one has dropped out, and we are still on eleven. And that is after the thirty-four times we have checked the ten, five, two and then one-day forecasts for the postcode that we are due to play in. 'Unbroken sunshine', it says, and our hearts leap a little. Even if it said 'showers', we would check every other weather app or site until we found one that promised fine conditions.

On the day of the match, we wake to the quiet thrill of anticipation. We get our kit bag ready and leave it by the front door for everyone to trip over. We rush through our morning tasks – the mowing, the compost, the dog walk – and we make ourselves sandwiches out of last night's remains. And, before we hop lightly into our cars, we reinforce our marriages by promising endless joyful winter afternoons at B&Q, or the garden centre, for we know that it is a price worth paying. Solitary confinement would be worth doing for a sunny weekend cricket match.

For a short time when we arrive at the ground, there is potential in every blade of grass, and every fold in the landscape. If you could stop the clock of life, you would do it here and now.

IN his autobiography, Donald Bradman devoted half a page to the Breeder's father's bowling. It had come to his attention in the summer of 1948, when the latter had dismissed the Don, caught Compton, for six in a match at Lords, achieving the alluring front-page headline in *The Times*, 'Bradman goes cheaply', in the process. He had then gone on to trap Len Hutton twice in a day in Oxford University's match against Yorkshire, before injuries blighted his career. He died never knowing that his own son could have reprised that headline hundreds of times over the next thirty years or so: 'Breeder goes cheaply'. It could be one of our straplines.

However, in terms of bowling pedigree, I mused, as the

Breeder went to his mark to deliver the first ball of the second over, you could filter the bloodline no purer than this. Whereas the Graduate was an intoxicating and explosive mix of sheer effort and brute force, the Breeder represented quiet, genetic perfection.

The church clock was striking the quarter hour when he bowled his first ball, a full and straight one that moved slightly away and which the batsman patted quietly to point, where it was collected by the Ginger. The politics and philosophy undergraduate from Exeter has a strong air of Jesus about him, with a long mane of ginger hair and beard to match, to the point where it is quite easy to imagine him clearing the money lenders out of the temple once he has dealt with the small matter of fielding the ball. He is the Graduate's younger brother, Al, and exudes a surprising, quiet competence given that he generally only plays a couple of times a year. He lobbed the ball back to the Breeder, who walked pensively back to his mark.

The next delivery was equally full, but wider, and the batsman carved it out towards the point boundary, where the Young Farmer was prowling. He is as close as we ever get to excellence, and does things with bat, ball and arm that leave the older players sighing with a mixture of inadequacy and respect. In our club, the youth field deep, as it is only they who can hurl the ball back into the keeper in the full, without needing half of the villagers of South Oxfordshire to relay it in for them.

Decades of breeding and guile went into the next ball, which moved away viciously from the right-hander when it pitched, and caught a thick outside edge in the direction of the Engineer at second slip. Maybe she was mulling over her day job of fixing submarines at the time, but her clutching hands got no closer to the ball than a foot, and it sped past her without having its progress interrupted in the slightest. It would be difficult for the average player to get their hands further away from the ball than she managed if they were trying to avoid it, let alone catch it.

It is a strange feature of our club that we seem to hide our most inept fielders in the cordon behind the bat, where the ring of steel metamorphoses into a ring of black holes. Commentary on cricket such as this, we have always felt, would be more appropriate if it were provided by someone with knowledge of quantum physics, such as Professor Brian Cox, rather than by *Test Match Special*.

The Engineer was our latest recruit, having heard about us and determined that we would be a more genial bunch than the women's cricket league side she currently played for. We thought momentarily of calling her the Human Colander, to go alongside her fellow kitchen implement in the form of the Sieve, but felt on reflection that it lacked originality, and that she had been put on this earth to do more than drain peas.

'I'm so sorry,' she called out.

'Don't worry. Well tried,' said the Breeder, dreaming of the sheep pens of the Usk Agricultural Show, whilst the Sieve quietly shared with her some of the more advanced techniques of dropping catches that he had uncovered along the way. Meanwhile, the Tree Hugger had thought of three more librarian puns involving the words 'volume', 'archive' and 'shelf', and was frantically signalling to me like a man who needs the toilet, or wants to be given a bowl.

The following two balls were exquisitely crafted by the Breeder, and treated with respect by the reprieved librarian. The sixth and final ball of the over was a horror, slow and short-pitched somewhere outside the leg stump, and the batsman did what anyone would do, even the Sieve, and brutalised it in the direction of the dreaming spires of Oxford a few miles away. If ever a ball deserved to go for eight, or ten, rather than a mere six, it was this one, and we had to admit that he had done it full justice.

However, Newton's first law states that 'every object will remain at rest or in uniform motion unless compelled to change its state by the action of an external force', and in-between the librarian's bat and those spires was the external force required in the bearded presence of the Beekeeper. Having seemed to all the world as being asleep on his feet (after all, the man worked nights in a fruit and veg business in Covent Garden, so this was two in the morning for him), he plucked it out of the air like a flycatcher takes an insect on the wing, and the Bodleian Library XI were eleven for two, after two overs.

How we had got to that point says much about our cricket. Eight respectable deliveries, two dropped catches and two wickets off comfortably the worst balls that had been bowled. The only thing that was missing was the eleventh player, who had written the fixture in his diary for the wrong day, and was even now belting up the A34 as fast as his car could go, his mind churning with the apologies he had been required to dish out to his wife and family when the call had come in from us at five to two, and with the excuses he would subsequently make to us on his arrival.

The Wealth Manager was no doubt highly competent at running the minutiae of the finances of ultra-high-net-worth individuals, but for his own part, he couldn't even run a bath. We knew for a fact that he was on first-name terms with the manager of the Lost and Found Office at Waterloo Station, but he was also one of the nicest people on earth, and 'nice' is the finest currency with which to settle apologies. Somewhere in the middle of the fifth over of the librarians' innings, he arrived at the ground, smiling and waving apologetically, but still comfortably the earliest he had arrived at a match all season.

Halfway through their innings, the Bodleian Librarians were struggling to make a competitive total, but then the young Library Assistant came in at number six, and things started to accelerate.

He was younger, thicker set and less studious than his colleagues, as if endless days spent rehoming heavy volumes of Descartes' *Passions of the Soul* from the lower to the upper reading rooms had bulked him out. He had the air of someone who might be a special constable at weekends, keeping the students of the town in order, and knowing what to do about it if that order was broken.

He smiled genially at the surrounding fielders, announced that he was 'crap' and that he would not detain us long, before launching the first ball he received from the Ginger clean over a neighbouring chestnut tree.

'Bugger me!' he announced cheerfully. 'How did that happen?'

The librarian at the other end frowned at the vocabulary, but applauded the shot.

We couldn't help him with how it had happened, but it was a shot that he repeated more than a handful of times against the inswingers of the Young Farmer, the outswingers of the Breeder, and the slow half-trackers that the Tree Hugger had made all his own over the years. Almost before we noticed, he was on 41, and his side had advanced to 160 for five, with a few overs in hand to give us a tricky chase in what would soon be the gathering autumnal gloom.

'Bowl yourself!' shouted the Graduate, and a chorus of voices joined in the clamour. Possibly the Library Assistant thought that this popular demand denoted some extraordinary skill on my part rather than the prosaic truth, which was that I was the worst bowler on earth, possibly further afield even, and they quite enjoyed watching me trying to complete any given over. I hadn't bowled for four years, but something about the ground, the company and the match situation persuaded me that now was the time.

I would like to say that I arranged the field, but I can't; the field arranged itself. They scattered to the furthest regions of the ground like the seed heads of a dandelion in the wind, and it was only by pathetic pleading that I managed eventually to persuade two of them to come in close enough to stop quick singles, not that the Library Assistant looked to be the quick-single type. The Graduate announced that deep mid on was where the catch would inevitably go, and he placed himself there in readiness for it.

Nearly 1,500 days had passed since I last turned my arm over, and muscle memory alone only barely managed to deliver a slow, high lob in the direction of the batsman. His eyes lit up, as he pondered momentarily into which of the three surrounding counties he should dispatch it. There was a ripe sound of leather on the sweet spot of willow, and the ball towered high above the ground, high enough and long enough for the Graduate to run a full thirty yards to cling onto it with the tips of his fingers just inside the boundary's edge.

One ball, one wicket, one event that defied the laws of reason. The eighteenth-century mathematician, Thomas Bayes, would have called it an example of marginal probability; everyone else called it pure bloody luck.

'Well bowled,' said the Breeder.

When all was said and done, it signalled the start of a mini collapse, and we were soon eating tea and cracking the odd book joke, knowing that we had the small matter of 171 runs to make to win the match.

I sent the Tree Hugger and the Graduate in first. This was

partly because they formed a cunning mixture of defence and attack, and partly because we were running a book at the time on run-outs, and I knew that this partnership produced by far the best chance of that happening, and therefore me getting my tenner stake back. After that, everyone contributed, but not at the rate that we needed to get comfortably over the line.

The Wealth Manager hit a cultured and elegant fifty, at which point we retired him and sent in the Beekeeper, then the Gun Runner, then the Engineer. With eight wickets down, and two overs left, we needed twenty-one runs to win the match, and not to lose more than one wicket to draw it, and there were the Ginger and I out there, with the Human Sieve ready to come in if a wicket fell in the interim.

As I waited for my first ball, I reflected on how close to perfection this situation was for a social cricketer like me. The asking rate was high enough to require one of us to be a hero, if we were to achieve it. There was one batsman to come and, even granting that it was the Sieve, this meant that the first one of us to get out wouldn't have actually lost the match.

Best of all, the skipper had lost count of which bowlers had used their allocation of overs, and all he could come up with now was an elderly bookish sort, who looked as if he would be more at home among the cartography and maps of the Weston library than bowling the penultimate over of a competitive cricket match.

The field spread and he bowled a nice, full-length ball, which I pulled behind square for four. Seventeen needed off eleven balls. I walked down the pitch like they do in proper cricket, hoping to meet the Ginger for an important-looking, mid-wicket conference; however, his mind was elsewhere, chatting to the bowler, and I wandered back alone, feeling ever so slightly diminished.

Of the two versions of me available to play the situation, I am sad to say that it was the delinquent holding the bat, whose concept of shot selection consisted of horrible leg-side heaves whatever the delivery, rather than strokes that were appropriate to the occasion. However, with one ball left, the Ginger and I had eked out enough ugly runs to need six off the final ball, and it was me facing.

Mythology requires the ball to have been smote high into the Oxfordshire sky and into a nearby garden before the victory celebrations. Mythology would be wrong. Instead, I bullied it to long on, and trotted through for the single to leave the match deservedly drawn.

As the last match of our long, hot English summer, it had contained just about everything. Competitiveness, brilliance, incompetence, suspense, hospitality and humour. Ahead of us was a French tour, and then the long dark nights of a northern winter, but for now, we were blessed to be here with each other, and with the librarians.

But it had not been like this more than six months ago. Not by a long chalk.

Privately, I had come a long way.

2 A Secret Plan

February

WINTER was hanging around like an ungrateful child, overstaying its welcome, and strewing the evidence of its presence around the house and garden. The cold and damp had become so much a part of our lives that we had grown to expect a grey and unchanged land each morning when we drew back the curtains. Yet, throughout this time, most of what we talked about was cricket and the coming summer.

At the end of the last season, I had started to feel my age. At fifty-seven, I felt privileged beyond measure still to be playing cricket, to be living a love affair with a sport that had begun for me forty-one years earlier. Equally, a tiny bit of me, the part that dreamed of producing an elegant cover drive that never really materialised, wondered whether I should call it a day. There is a distinct moment when the plucky trier becomes an embarrassment to his teammates, and the trick is to call time before it happens. Perhaps this season should be my last, I thought, before I put away my old kit bag in the attic, and become an umpire.

The Graduate had recently moved to London for work, and he had joined an indoor winter cricket league. For him, it was a time of discovery. Indoor cricket was effectively a completely different sport from the one he was used to playing, and his various subcontinental and Australian teammates pointed out with infinite patience that his brand of aerial smash-and-grab cricket didn't really work in a new discipline where precision was everything, and that keeping the ball on the floor brought rich rewards. It turned out he was a respectful listener.

'This Sri Lankan bloke has taught me a new back-of-the-hand slower ball,' he announced one snowy Saturday breakfast, when he had come home for the weekend. 'Will you come down to the nets and let me try it on you?'

I looked outside at the Arctic greyness, and then back at him.

'Why would I want to do that?'

What he was asking was technically possible, in that the outdoor nets of the Midhurst cricket club stayed up all year, but without a shred of obvious attraction. I told him so in colourful terms, but eventually his persistence paid off. There seemed to be something faintly heroic about the idiocy of a middle-aged man having grenades hurled down at him by his son in the February sleet, while others were at home in the warm reading the papers. It was a continuum of an old family motto to the effect that you very rarely regretted what you did, only what you didn't do.

That's the thing about sport: it can't always be a highlights package. The golfer drills bucket after bucket of balls down the range, day in and day out, come rain, hail or sun, just so that he can dream of one day walking down the eighteenth, clutching his cap, and smiling smugly at the adoring crowd. And here, so much lower down the sporting food chain that it almost hurts, the Graduate was making good his need to practise, so that he could get incrementally better, whilst I was agreeing to it in a last-ditch attempt to stop the slide into competitive futility.

To its true lover, cricket is a twelve-month mistress, and the dozen or so games played in the summer merely the tip of a very large iceberg. By dragging me out into the February dank, the Graduate was simply articulating the old truth that there is never a right time not to be thinking about cricket.

A man is blessed when one of his sons shares one of his passions, doubly so when both of them do. Initially, in the early and mid-teenage years, all the momentum had come from me: asking them to play cricket as a favour, not as an order; inviting their friends along to play, so the long phoneless periods out in the middle wouldn't be quite so boring for them. It also involved praising them when things went right and consoling them when they didn't, letting them bat early, bowl often and field close, in order to give time for cricket's gentle tendrils to encircle them before they even noticed. With the Graduate it had worked; with his younger brother, the Ginger, the jury was still out.

But for now, the Graduate and I were merely the designated survivors of the White Hunter's previous season.

Of the original eleven White Hunters from that July afternoon thirty-odd years ago, there were only three remaining: the Tree Hugger, the Land Agent and me.

We had formed, if that is the word, to give a game to someone else who had recently formed a club, and wanted to see how it all worked. *They* came from London with the cool professionalism of people for whom cricket was a finely honed art; they had the skills, they had the coaching, and they had the attitude. Actually, above all, they had the jargon.

We, on the other hand, came from the valleys and farms of Hampshire and Sussex; and we knew, as soon as we clapped eyes on each other in whites for the first time, that incompetence would be our friend, and low expectations our benchmark. Between us we had many sports, and many activities that we perhaps excelled at, so it was chronically disappointing that cricket wasn't one of them.

Time passed. We consisted of farmers and factors, salesmen and soldiers, land agents and lawyers. It wasn't called downtime in those days, but if it had been, our downtime would have been darts and bar billiards in the Thomas Lord at West Meon, real ale straight out of the barrel at the Flower Pots at Cheriton, and quiz nights anywhere that would take us.

Season after season, we had survived partly through the variety we provided into otherwise predictable lives, and partly through the sheer bloody-minded determination of the Tree Hugger and me to keep it all going. For we knew that if we didn't, the terrifying result would be the personal loss of a passport into a game that we both adored with an irrational passion, but that we weren't good enough to be invited to play otherwise.

'YOU pad up,' said the Graduate.

We set his old Slazenger cricket bag on its end as a makeshift wicket, and the damp morning dog-walkers walked behind us in amused surprise. Droplets of mist hung off the netting, and dew saturated the grass around the bowler's mark.

In terms of the style of the Graduate's batting, the apple hadn't fallen very far from its tree, but his bowling was so much better than mine that it was almost impossible to believe we were related. He had learned to move it both ways in the right conditions, and he chose a ball out of the bag, so rough that even David Warner, a player with the almost heroic distinction of being more disliked than were the Chappell brothers back in the seventies, would be embarrassed by the state of it. I had learned nothing, on the other hand, other than to try to play for the first time in glasses, to give me a chance of picking what exactly was leaving his hand twenty-two yards away.

His first outside ball of the season passed a yard outside my off stump, and I allowed it through with an exaggerated leave, if only to make the passive-aggressive point that he would have to bowl a lot straighter to interest me. The man who had fixed our boiler, when it gave in a few weeks before, stood behind the net to watch the action with his patient dog.

'I thought you said that you could play cricket,' he said inevitably, as I slashed a top edge off the next ball into the back netting. I considered a humorous response, but then remembered I still hadn't paid his bill, and thought better of it.

The third passed the same distance outside leg, as the Graduate's cold hands were finding it hard to calibrate his direction-finding radar.

Our net cricket was always a game within a game, unequal, as only one of us could actually bowl. The Graduate, who had not shown the slightest interest in cricket whilst at school, had compensated for his lack of education by poring over YouTube training videos night after night in his time at university. The research reaped rich rewards for him, as his Wild-Man-of-Borneo approach to the game was gently subsumed into a passable consistency with both bat and ball; it was generally agreed that no one in the club's history had ever hit a ball harder, or with more murderous effect. More importantly, it was an expression of an uncomplicated lack of fear that is the sole preserve of people who haven't yet had their first tax bill, or mortgage payment.

It had never once occurred to me that I would one day be a father, until I was about to become one. It wasn't that I wanted to avoid fatherhood, but in my twenties, children had been the sole preserve of people who drove Volvos, booked village halls for parties, and worried a lot about air pollution. Worse still, they made my friends boring, and stopped them doing adventurous things with us at weekends. And that was before they even started banging on about academic excellence, or achievements at the Pony Club.

But then parenthood sort of crept up on us, and we found ourselves one May afternoon staring down at a bundle that contained our son, wondering why they hadn't given us an instruction manual when we left the hospital.

'Do you think he's a left-hander?' asked the Tree Hugger. 'How early can you tell? It would be good to have one of those on the books in a few years.'

Three years later he was joined by a brother, and the Tree Hugger, in agreeing to be a godfather, told me that he had the wrist of a leg spinner, and that all would be well in consequence.

Now our first baby was a tall, heavily bearded young man, and after another few minutes of net practice, I watched him scoop the ball up and walk back to his mark, with his familiar, no-nonsense trudge.

'I'll give you six more balls,' he said. 'You've got to get sixteen runs to win, and one wicket left.'

I carved the first, an outswinger, high over where point would have been, and in my imagination it crashed into the boundary boards a second or two later.

'Twelve to get,' I called to him, as I lobbed the ball back up the net.

'Sixteen, actually,' he said. 'You were caught by the sweeper I put out there a couple of balls before.' It was a bit of theatre we had done between us a hundred times before, and it meant that no one ever fully won or lost. Second slip miraculously becomes fly slip becomes third man, depending on the shot just played, and everyone goes home happy.

The next ball was as fast as he could bowl, straight and infinitely drivable, and I duly smacked it high into the netting above where he had stopped. If I had played that shot out in the middle during a match, it would comfortably have been one of the best I had ever hit.

'Six,' he said. 'Shot!' He looked at me for a while, part proud child, part outraged bowler, both parts thinking of something to say. 'You should practise more often.'

Much as he didn't like his bowling being hit to all parts, he quite liked his father to do well. He walked back to his mark and bowled a repeat, which I flicked elegantly behind square, wondering as I did so why I couldn't play like this when it really mattered. We agreed it was worth two runs, leaving me four to get off the last two balls.

I decided two things about the penultimate ball in advance of it being bowled. First, that he would try and spear a yorker in at my feet; second, that I would premeditate a charge down the wicket to make it into a full toss and hoick it into the imaginary grandstand out over deep long on, where a large lady was bagging up her dog's recent business.

When it came down to it, what he actually bowled was a fast, waist-high full toss outside the leg stump. Nine times out of ten, I would have swayed out of the way and let it crash harmlessly into the back netting. But my blood was up, and I was hitting the ball cleaner, and harder, than I had for about a quarter of a century. So I stepped into the path of the ball, and took it on, only in the event managing to top-edge it from the bat into my jaw, at which point my world went dark.

I sunk to my knees, dropped the bat on the ground, and held my hand up to the point of impact.

In the seconds that followed, the Graduate fretted that I was concussed, whilst I was only interested in how many teeth I might have lost.

'I'm so sorry. So, so sorry,' he repeated as some sort of mantra. He was genuinely distraught.

'It's my fault,' I said, spitting blood through my batting gloves as I staggered to my feet. 'I should have left it alone. I'm not quick enough to do that sort of stuff anymore.'

Blood never looks great on the white of gloves, pads and cricket sweaters.

'You're in a shit state,' the Graduate said comfortingly. 'I think you'd better scrub up before we go home.'

What he meant was that under no circumstances should my wife, Caroline, be allowed to see me until I was as presentable as medically possible. Cleanliness, plus a plausible excuse: those were the two things that were needed. In default of them, both our lives could quickly become more complicated.

GENERALLY, my body was functional for its age.

The unsaid deal between me and it was that I would fill

it with exactly what I wanted — crisps, San Miguel, digestive biscuits, for example — but that in return I would exercise it prodigiously and give it occasional breaks. For each of the last six years, I had made it run or row the same number of miles as there were years in the date, a slightly pointless activity that could by definition only ever get worse as we aged together. But this process kept its automotive system ticking along; more a beaten-up Volkswagen Passat than a purring old Ferrari to be sure, but still ticking along.

However, in the five phases of active life, I had reached the third, the one that mirrors British players in week two of the Wimbledon Championships, delighted still to be an active participant in proceedings.

At the end of the previous cricket season, I had uttered my normal mantra about it probably being 'time for me to pack it in', something that was usually as dishonest as it was unlikely, and calculated to recruit a sympathy vote that simply didn't exist. But I was coming close to believing it, this time. The throwing arm, always the first thing to go, had duly gone. The bowling arm hadn't gone, in the sense that something that is not there in the first place can't really go anywhere. The batting was as hollow and predictable as a Hugh Grant rom-com, fed, as he was, with the occasional brilliant one-liner.

The only thing that was left was my captaincy, which got better as my cricket deteriorated. I simply spent less time trying to please people and learned more about who not to let anywhere near the action at important times of the game. It didn't make me any more popular, but it got things done.

After a ten-minute visit to the café bathroom, I nursed the coffee the Graduate had bought me.

'It's a bit of a sign,' I said. 'I need to umpire from now on. I'm too bloody slow for batting.'

He looked at me. 'Rubbish. Buy a helmet. That way, when you get hit in the head, it will just ring in your ears.'

And then, after a thoughtful pause, he added, 'You could always learn to bat, I suppose.'

I ignored him.

'It's not the getting old, or being hit, that I mind about. It's being rubbish. I don't want to stop, but I think it might be better. And I will probably get used to it.'

This was fraudulent stuff, but not entirely so; this time I was really beginning to believe that the seemingly endless run of disappointments was finally tipping the scales.

I had seen these people a thousand times before, the frail army of veteran cricketers who fail to understand when their time is up. I had watched them descending down the batting order over the years, like a deflating child's balloon slowly sliding down the wall long after the party has finished, and I had noticed them retreat from the interesting fielding positions in front of the bat to safe and inconsequential ones behind it. Until one day they all finally fetched up at deep fine leg, where they could do the least damage, part of a terracotta army of sixty-somethings stuck in the ground three-quarters of the way back to the boundary.

But I had never really noticed how they always seemed to be smiling.

The Graduate stared into his coffee for a second and said out of the blue, 'Maybe you're right. Time to put your feet up. Time to let the new generation drive it on.'

This was beginning to sound less like a sympathetic hearing for an injured father, and more like a hostile takeover bid. Was he being serious, or was this his version of humouring a small child by taking a contrary view to the one they expected? Either way, I didn't have the energy to argue, so I tried to sound enigmatic.

'We'll see,' I said. But the whole left side of my face was throbbing, and I just wanted to be in a dark room somewhere.

March

'BETWEEN the idea and the reality,' said T.S. Eliot, 'falls the shadow.' He knew what he was talking about.

Heart eventually won the battle with head over the matter of whether to go on playing or not, as it was always going to, but in the weeks after being hit on the face, I spent quite a lot of time realising it was up to me, and not fate, to present myself back on the cricket pitch in as competent form as I could.

On a scale of one to ten, where one is total incompetence and ten is Bradman, I decided I would like to get to at least three; that point where the level of my skills would pass under the radar as a topic of conversation. And to get even that far, I had to do something positive, rather than wait for it all to happen. If I was going to start the new season as the kind of sporting demigod that I now envisaged, quite a lot of water needed to flow under the metaphorical bridge. Or, to be more exact, flexibility, robustness, skill and mental strength were all queueing up to be improved, and quick.

I had a grand total of two months in which to achieve this. Also, I saw no reason to share this sudden conversion with other members of the team, especially the younger ones, so it had to be done in secret.

This was partly to maximise the splendour of the moment my butterfly emerged from its chrysalis, and partly as a giant insurance policy against the eventuality of it all not working, and no one noticing anything different. There was no need to strew banana skins in my own path, and to end up looking a prat.

I mentioned the matter to Caroline later that evening.

'You need a plan,' she said sleepily. 'And probably some lessons. And a helmet. And to sort your hip out. And possibly not to bang on about it too much if you want it to be a secret.' I was keen for her to avoid pointing out that it was not rocket science, as people only ever did that if they thought a very simple thing was in danger of being complicated by a very stupid person.

'It's not exactly rocket science,' she said, and went upstairs to bed.

CLAUSEWITZ'S first principle of war, I remembered having drilled into me as a young soldier about a millennium ago, was to understand what constituted a good outcome. If this was to be the Renaissance season I had in mind, then it needed a series of ambitious aims, wrapped up in a statement of intent. I sat down one night and jotted them down in the pad I kept in my desk for late-night idiocies:

> *Finish the season with a batting average of over 30* (the previous year, it had struggled to get to 12), *including a 50* (none for four years), *and win fifty per cent or more of all our matches* (last year, we won 2 out of 17).

Clausewitz then goes on to opine, 'Make best use of the few means at your disposal, never waste time, and use the entire force with utmost energy and focus.' Although he might not have had the White Hunter Cricket Club in mind when he wrote this all down back in 1812, there is no question that he meant it to be durable. I noted down the basis of the plan as it emerged in my mind:

1. *Repair the body. At least make it as good as it possibly can be without a hip replacement, or a miracle.* For this, I needed treatment, and some sort of regime.

2. *Repair the attitude. At least help it to shed the belief that every ball I faced would be my last* For this, I probably needed a sporting psychologist.

3. *Repair the cricket.* For this, I needed some technical coaching.

4. *Get the gear.* For this, I would simply need to visit a sports shop.

I couldn't legislate for the unplayable ball, or the misbehaving pitch, but I could at least get to the beginning of the season as prepared as I could be, even if preparation was a concept with which my body was largely unfamiliar.

I emailed the Tree Hugger:

Forget that bit about me giving up cricket and forget that you and I were ever incompetent. I have a plan, and it involves you, expensive coaching and five or six nights of intrigue. But it also involves beer, brilliance and, dare I say it, awards in the autumn for player of the season. That's how good it is. Call me in the morning. R.

Considering the matter as good as sorted already, and with one eye on yet another principle of war (economy of effort), I put the aim in a sealed envelope and headed to bed to sleep, perchance to dream about cricket bats and rocket science.

A journey of a thousand miles starts with a single step, as the saying goes, and so I began by investing £95 into a fourteen-week yoga course, every Tuesday evening at a local village hall.

For the first five minutes, it looked to me like yoga and I were going to get along fine, as the instructor told us to lie down, relax, and listen to our bodies. Granted, my body hadn't got much to say, and, anyway, it was under strict instructions not to make any of those extraneous noises that might be a by-product of complete physical relaxation. It took me three weeks to pluck up enough courage to find out that the problem of wind is dealt with during the noisy bits. As with most sport, it's all in the timing.

Still, my body was happy enough to be in a darkened room, and even more so to be encouraged to tune out to the sound of whale music. Which it duly did.

Fifteen minutes later, however, it was all *Down Dog, Plank, Cat, Cow, Warrior One* and *Seated Forward Pose*. My body, which had all the flexibility of a North Korean military parade, was suddenly being asked to do things that it had hitherto imagined only got done in California, and then only by people who lived on a diet of chia seeds, anti-depressants and tantric sex.

My presence as an incompetent male in a room full of women, who all seemed to be able to fold their bodies double, was a strange one. If they had been blokes, they would have laughed at me, which would have been fine; as it was, they fixed me with empowering, sisterly smiles, and willed me to amount to more than a Victorian parody of manliness.

The reason that men fundamentally don't do stuff like yoga, I thought to myself, is that there is no excitement before it, no competitiveness during it and no beer after it. Participants simply turn up, quietly bend bits of their body in half, and then head back to a spotless kitchen to watch *MasterChef*.

My first session came to an undignified end when my back gave in during an attempt at *Little Cobra*. In previous years, that would have been that, and I would never have gone again. But for the time being it was serious, and I rather hoped that I was in for the duration. I could pause, but I couldn't stop.

Then it was to the hospital for an X-ray on my hip and to the pharmacy for painkillers that would tide me through the rough bits, until such time that they did something about it. Twice a day, I lay on the floor and did hip-rotator exercises under the baleful instruction of a humourless YouTube doctor and his unfeasibly mobile assistant called Ryan. Then I started doing daily sit-ups on the basis that they helped build stomach muscles, which, in turn, then helped to diminish belly fat.

When the Tree Hugger and I met up in the secrecy of the Harrow Inn at Steep to discuss the coming season, the 'c' word manifested itself almost immediately. For most of the thirty years we had been running the club, 'coaching' was simply a thing that happened to other people, a surrender of basic principles that should be treated with due scorn, even as the perpetrators helped themselves to fifty after fifty off the White Hunter bowling.

When we said that someone looked as though they had been coached during the winter, we had meant it as an insult, and we meant it to sting.

Not any more we didn't, though. In a conversion so complete that it wouldn't have been out of place on the road to Damascus, we agreed that secret lessons from true professionals were what we both needed, and we duly celebrated with more beer and a packet of pork scratchings.

Sometimes it was hard to remember that this was about

getting better at cricket but, twinge by twinge, ache by ache, bit by tiny bit, I was giving my body something that it hadn't had since it belonged to a recruit soldier nearly forty years before, something called preparation. The body was starting to repair itself, but it would be stretching the truth to say that it was enjoying the process.

After about a week, I received an email from the Graduate: 'Thinking of coming back this weekend. Do you fancy a couple of nets?'

'Not right now,' I lied. 'I'm not going to practise at all this year.' The plan was for him to be stunned by my wonderfulness, but only when I chose to reveal it.

My Google search for 'best cricket bat money can buy' led me inexorably to the Gray-Nicolls Legend, at a round £1,000. I read greedily of the 'mid-blade that is ideally suited for front and back-foot play' and the 'concave sculpting to give professional pick-up and balance', and I was immediately in a world of cricketing porn. The left side of my brain was admitting sadly that buying this bat, even if I could afford it, would not make the slightest difference to the outcomes of my cricket, whilst the dominant right side was screaming: 'It doesn't matter. Buy the bloody thing. See even now how it makes you dribble with excitement.'

I moved down a notch, through the Salix (£675), and the GM Player Edition (£615), until I gradually arrived back at the top end of the world I actually recognised and could possibly justify. My old Kookaburra Genesis had served me rather better than I had served it, but it was beginning to show its age by now, in a series of cracks at the base, and splintering on the side. I took it down to the sports shop late one Saturday afternoon and asked the delighted owner to adjudicate.

After he had confirmed that it was past praying for, I headed into familiar retail territory (like backing the second favourite in a horse race, or buying the second-cheapest wine on the menu) by settling on the second-most expensive bat on his shelf. It was the direct descendant of the one that had given me nearly a decade of service, and it was reduced to from £200 to £120. Then, as an afterthought based on the deal I had made with my wife, I bought myself a helmet.

I stood outside the shop and felt myself falling in love all over again. A new bat in the hands of an old cricketer is the embodiment of positive thinking, and it is the triumph of hope over experience. It is like a first date, where the days ahead are full of uncomplicated promise, and where the only thing to pay for is the first round of drinks. Aristotle once said that 'happiness depends upon ourselves', but he was wrong. Without so much as a cricket net anywhere near him in Macedonia, how could the old philosopher have known otherwise?

There is something so elementally satisfying about a new, pristine cricket bat that even the act of describing it defiles it. The light-sanded grain of a three-pound chunk of twenty-year-old English willow, as yet untouched by ball, glove or oil even, is a thing of beauty and craftsmanship. It is a ship of dreams, because it has not yet been acquainted with failure. Failure would come in her own good time (and she knew full well where to find me), but for now, I was a knight of Camelot with his own Excalibur, heading back to his car at the far end of the Waitrose car park.

When I got home, I showed it to Caroline, and watched the battle rage across her face between the keeper of the housekeeping budget for whom this was frivolity writ large, and the working artist who recognised a true masterpiece when she saw it.

'It is rather wonderful,' she agreed. 'Does it come with instructions?'

Later on, there was an email from the Young Farmer, another

cornerstone of our youth policy: 'I gather you aren't doing nets this year. Have you been taken ill, or something? Get a grip. Everyone does nets.'

He was right. We do. But mine were going to be very different nets to the ones that the Young Farmer and the Graduate were used to: physically in another county, but financially and aspirationally in a different galaxy.

'No. Probably giving them a miss this year. Hope they go well.'

A man could get used to this acting business.

3 The Pathway of Four Improvements

Late March

THE thin pulse of ambition that flickers on and off in most middle-aged men persuaded the Tree Hugger not to ignore my email, but to embrace it, and we duly met in the secrecy of the back room of the Harrow in Steep, to plan our training regime. The centre point of the Venn Diagram, one circle of which was the Tree Hugger's pedantic practicality and the other my own hopelessly broad-canvas organising, emerged as a three-point plan:

- PHASE 1: We would attend one White Hunter CC net, more to sow the seeds of deception than to learn anything useful, or new.

- PHASE 2: We would then do three private sessions of regional coaching at Arundel Castle Cricket School, with an old county pro who had helped propel Sussex to their first ever championship in 2003. This would take us back to basics.

- PHASE 3: Finally, we would do three further sessions at Hampshire's Rose Bowl training school, this time with a current county batting coach. This would thread into the fabric of our game the brutality and inventiveness of modern Twenty20 cricket, so that we would emerge as slightly stiffer versions of Jos Buttler.

And we would stick exclusively to batting. Fielding was simply something that you did on the day, when the occasion arose, and it either worked or it didn't; besides, you couldn't coach a creaking, fourteen-stone body suddenly to be an agile, eleven-stone one, which was what fielding really needed. And bowling, especially my bowling, was simply too much for a coach to deal with in five or six years, let alone five or six sessions. To make any difference to my bowling, a man would need limitless time, ambition, patience and budget. It would be easier to turn base metal into gold.

We started by attending the first White Hunter club net of the year. These pre-season nets are always moist with leaking testosterone, and consequently next to useless for practical training.

Overweight, out of condition bowlers, who have not thrown anything larger than a fuse for six months, suddenly try to bowl at the speed of Malcolm Marshall, and wonder why they can't move the next day. Normally obdurate batsmen behave like skittish cattle let out onto the spring pastures after a long winter indoors and, dance down the wicket, flinging their pale forearms through the line of a ball that has whistled past them a mere half an hour before. The Land Agent then misbehaves with the bowling machine until it is firing down inswingers at eighty-five miles per hour to men whose accumulated injuries have only just allowed them to make it to the net session.

Whether they have been hiding away in offices all through the close season, or sneaking off to indoor leagues, everyone convinces themselves in the pub afterwards that the cricketing situation is impossibly good, and the prognosis deliciously promising. Time after time, we tell ourselves that this coming season is the one on which the sun will never set, that this time round we will all be Corinthians.

'I thought that you and the Tree Hugger weren't going to do nets any more,' said the Young Farmer, sidling hopefully up to where the round was being bought.

'We weren't,' I said, 'but we took pity. It's the price of leadership.' He looked at me quizzically, but then in the reflection of the mirror behind the bar as I settled up, I noticed him raise his eyebrows at the Graduate. They had seen it all before.

Three days later, the Tree Hugger and I presented ourselves to the Arundel coach, Brian.

'You don't know what you have let yourself in for,' the Tree Hugger told him apologetically, but it was clear that the challenge of altering the course of our combined one hundred and twenty years of mediocrity fascinated the coach rather than daunted him.

Brian examined our stances, our position, and the way we held our bats.

'You're both starting with your bat too far from your body. Which means it will come down naturally swinging into the on side. Which can be risky.' We duly clasped our hands to our chests, like nuns in a mountain convent.

'You're starting the backswing too low. Make a hinge, and come down from a height.' We came down from a height and made hinges of our elbows.

'Your heads are falling slightly over to the right.' So we held our heads erect and proud, like veterans at the Cenotaph.

He started with gentle chuck-downs, and complimented each of us on the way we watched the ball. 'I've had much worse than you in here,' he said, 'at younger than half your age.' It was faint praise perhaps, but when your sporting ability has crawled out of the primordial soup, faint praise is worth rubies. It is also all you are ever going to get.

It's called *andragogy*, the theory of teaching people to do things who are themselves old enough to be expected to know how to do them anyway. Fundamentally, you are doing this stuff because you want to, not because your parents are telling you to. It is why adult education works so well, in theory at least, and particularly when it concerns males, and spherical things. And, as the coaching continued, I came to realise how empowering it was for a fifty-eight-year-old even to be involved in this process, let alone benefiting from it. I was breathing excellence, and that was good enough for me.

On the third session, we brought along the Wealth Manager. Secrecy was one thing, but the ruinous cumulative price of these sessions was quite another, and we decided that we needed to amortise the cost a little as we went along. He was returning to cricket after a four-year lay-off that featured a magnificent cornucopia of injuries and illnesses that could have filled a medical dictionary. So it was pleasing to see how close to human he looked as he turned up for the training. For the best part of half a decade, we had reckoned on not seeing him in whites again.

From the first confident, defensive push, he was annoyingly good. His stance, according to the coach, was blameless, his balance exquisite. A career of managing other people's money had morphed into an unfussy way of managing his own batsmanship, and he took to the coaching like a duck to water. Dearly as we may have loved him, it was as if the school swot had come back from a protracted sick leave, and immediately recited the first thirty pages of *Beowulf* to the delight of the English teacher.

'Hands a bit far from the body?' I offered helpfully to the coach.

'Head not quite over the ball?' asked the Tree Hugger.

'You could learn a lot from him,' said the coach, which rather settled the matter.

Bit by bit, he walked us through what we had long since forgotten, in the Tree Hugger's case, or never really known, in mine. Play the ball under the eyes; bend the front leg for the front-foot shots; head and shoulder leading; watch the ball all the way onto the bat; keep the eyes level; adjust to the line of the ball.

Whether it was looking good was anyone's guess, but it was certainly starting to feel good. And with the good feeling came a sense of empowerment. And with empowerment, came the age-old need for beer. Empowerment is like that: once you acquire it, you have to accept where it leads you. We took the Wealth Manager to the pub, and explained our little subterfuge.

'I'm in,' he said.

Early April

THERE were many differences, but it was the quality of sound that really distinguished them.

In net number five, stood a tall, left-handed batsman, who had scored the small matter of 12,000-plus runs in more than 150 Test matches, at an average of a shade under 50, and with a top score of 294. In nearly a century and a half of Test cricket history, he had worked his own modest, uncomplicated way to the very top of the professional tree.

Here in the training nets, the ball came off his bat with either a languid *pop*, when he chose to go back and across and defend out into the covers, or a rifle crack, if he decided to cut or pull it with force to the notional boundary. He exuded competence, and whatever else it is that really good professionals exude, but had the air of a man who would rather have been anywhere other than the Ageas Rose Bowl at Southampton on Day Four of a rain-affected county match against Hampshire.

He was called Alastair Cook, and he opened the batting for England.

In net number six, stood the short, right-handed and bespectacled Human Sieve, the White Hunter wicket-keeper/batsman. The Sieve sold industrial dishwashers for a living and it wasn't simply that he was bad at cricket, it was that he had personally redefined awfulness. Regular oppositions, who loved him as much as we did, would arrive at our ground and check first if the Sieve was playing. And not only because they felt his presence would make their own victory more likely, but because sometimes you need to break out of the ordinariness of life.

The previous summer, after twenty years of trying, he had

finally reached double figures in an individual innings for the very first time, by virtue of a sumptuous edge off a full and quick delivery down to the fine leg boundary. There, on that school pitch outside Petersfield, it was one of those 'stop the clocks and throw the dog a juicy bone' moments that everyone present will remember for the rest of their days. Others may laugh, but there were tears in the eyes of his teammates as they applauded him and acknowledged his raised bat that sunny June afternoon

He possessed two shots, each of which he would deploy in a predetermined sequence, no matter what ball was bowled at him: a waft outside the off stump, and a short-armed hoick to leg. He had a career batting average of one and a quarter runs per innings. But we had recruited the Sieve to these training sessions, because he made us happy, and we wanted more for him than for each short innings to end up with a trudge back to the pavilion.

And, by the end of the session that had started alongside Alastair Cook, there was no question that he had started to hit the ball more often than it hit him, which was progress indeed. At times, he even looked like he was playing cricket, and the Tree Hugger and I told him so. For in many ways the Sieve was the canary in the coalmine of White Hunter cricket and if he thrived, as far as we were concerned, we thrived. In the vivid imagination of our club scriptwriting, the glory days, when the Sieve would get amongst an opposition bowling attack or rescue us from a really dire position, were only just around the corner.

Our caravan of professional coaching, which had moved west down the coast from Arundel to the Rose Bowl at Southampton, had drawn more of the older players into its web. Although this had quite a lot to do with sharing out the cost, it was also an expression of subversive hope from an age group that was no longer expected to get better at things; merely to manage the decline. The way I was beginning to see it, the pathway of four improvements on which I was embarked was not only about the potential excellence of my cricket, but also a life-affirming statement of the ability of an old bloke to get better at things generally, and not to subside into the habitual bitterness of age.

We even allowed the Land Agent along, on the condition that he didn't move sets of stumps sideways while no one was looking, or try and get into a car race to the M27 roundabout once the session had finished.

And as with the Wealth Manager, the deal with the Sieve, the Land Agent and the others was that no one below the age of thirty was to hear a squeak about it.

WHILE the world outside started to green up and dry out, the season was emerging from the gloom of winter, and beginning to be more reality than pipe dream, accompanied by its own rites of rebirth.

The final touches were put to the fixture list, which was then circulated; new kit was purchased to replace what had gone astray or was falling to pieces; and players were exhorted to part with £60 for annual membership, so that we could at least start the season financially in credit. Personal kit was retrieved from attics and cupboards, dusted down and stowed ready for the first game. Negotiations with other family members started in earnest, and they would carry on all season.

In our world, oppositions select and deselect themselves, as we do with them. All clubs mutate, sometimes in sympathy with the way we are developing, sometimes not: everything depends on what is important to them, and what they want from a game of cricket. Consistent with always wanting to play as well as we can, a pecking order of our club's needs and wants from an opposition looks something like this:

1. A complete absence of disruptive, aggressive, or argumentative idiots.

2. An absence, if not a complete absence, of confrontation. Some of our best moments have been during personal duels, but they can rapidly stop being entertaining.

3. An understanding that a player, particularly a bowler, recruited from two or three levels up, can quickly ruin a game if not left at home, or at least handled imaginatively.

4. An appreciation of, and access to, beautiful or at least interesting grounds.

5. Taking turns to organise and host matches.

6. A quiet determination to get as close to twenty-two players as possible climbing into their cars at the end of the match, having had a good day.

7. A love of the game, and a genuine desire to do the right thing by it.

A couple of years shy of his sixtieth birthday, and given a little luck with health, a man like me might have fifty matches left in him as the clock ticked out. It was vital that they were well spent. A match not enjoyed was far worse than a match not played at all. And, after this long winter, we were only days away from the first game.

Of my list of four categories of self-improvement, I had already started tackling, with some energy, the body, the technicality of cricket, and the gear. Were it not for the complete absence of progress on the fourth – the attitude – I felt that I would be halfway there.

On the morning of our first match, I found myself on a couch considering unhelpful thoughts and internal battles. I had signed up with a sports psychologist called Jo, and serendipity had arranged that her first, early-morning session with me coincided with the start of our season.

'We'll begin by looking at your sporting history, and what you want out of it in the future,' she had emailed a few days before. What I wanted out of it was much simpler, and more impressive, than what had gone before. I had never been to a psychologist, and was rather over-excited about its potential effect, and the timescale that I thought it could be achieved in. I longed to lie on that couch and feel the warm winds of improvement wafting across my face.

The way I saw it, I would morph into one of those annoying, slightly overweight ex-Cambridge cricket blues, who would play once a year in their faded I Zingari sweater and score endless runs, at the same time looking as though they didn't want to be there. Each one a city banker, and each one called Giles.

'The problem is simple,' I explained. 'Every ball I have ever faced in my life I think is going to be my last. That fact informs and predicts what I then always do, which is to try to hit the ball into next week. At which point, often as not, I get out. It just becomes a self-fulfilling prophecy.'

She asked me why I thought this was, and I came up with a sense of the inevitable as my answer.

'I do not feel that I can control the outcome,' I told her. 'I am locked in a rinse-and-spin cycle of predestination, as far as cricket is concerned, and I've lost the telephone number of the mechanic.'

I thought that this was quite funny, and rather beautifully expressed, but she moved on quickly.

'What is going through your mind when the bowler is walking back to his mark?'

Jo knew about cricket; she treated the Surrey Youth Squad, amongst others.

'Too much,' I admitted. 'What ball is going to come down at me. Whether my partner at the other end is alert. Whether we have put the urn on for tea. Tomorrow's meeting. Brexit.'

'Then what happens?'

I told her, and we talked about focus, about emptying the mind, being in the moment. We also talked about physical fear, how I had felt it ever since I had head-butted that ball from Tom back in January. Fear. That's not something that grown men like to talk about. So I reminded myself about the promise to see this all through, and told her the truth.

She talked about the brain, and its limbic system, and how it governs behaviour, motivation and emotion. 'It's the bit that is offering you the options of "fight", "fly" or "freeze" when you are in a stressful, dangerous situation. You need it to survive, and it will ultimately decide whether what you are embarked on is a challenge, which is obviously a good thing, or a threat, which isn't.'

As I packed up to go, I asked her, 'Just give me one tip for this evening.' Even if it was a course of sessions, the child in me wanted immediate gratification.

'Before each shot, ask the question, am I being a good coach to myself.'

'What's a good outcome for you tonight?' she added, as I

walked down her driveway. I thought about it. It wasn't about the unplayable ball, or even the runs.

'When I'm out, I just want to be out to a shot I don't regret.'

It was a modest aim, but I would have come a long way if I actually achieved it.

SHAKESPEARE once said something about there being a tide in the affairs of men that, if taken at the flood, leads on to fortune. What he meant, loosely, is that you need to get on with it if it's heading on the right course; otherwise all previous work has been wasted. With body, kit, technique and brain all tilting in the right direction, I felt good as I drove over to Winchester for the first match of the season. And with the Tree Hugger cycling in Italy, the Graduate stuck in his office in London and the Wealth Manager being especially diligent in the money-managing world, it was left to the Human Sieve, the Land Agent and me to put our secret coaching into practice to the delighted surprise, we hoped, of our teammates.

We were a young side playing an evening beer match, our 369th in all, against a village opposition called Crawley. Over the years, we had won more than we had lost here, but that progression had been rudely reversed the previous year, when they turned out to have broken all conventions by setting in place a regime of winter nets.

As the skipper and I walked out for the toss, I prayed to the God of two-headed coins to allow me to win, and to ask them to bat first. This, I felt, would allow us to size up the chase, and set the scene for twilight heroics a couple of hours later. I called wrong, and he asked us to bat.

'Are you still bowling yourself?' he asked me, on our way back from the square.

'Probably not.' But I could sense his nervousness, for it was only a few years since I had recorded my best-ever bowling figures there. 'Hip's playing up a bit.'

'Shame,' he said. 'The boys were all rather hoping you would.' He thought for a moment and then added, 'I'm not really sure your kind of bowling needs a working hip, does it?'

I ignored the barb, and selected our oldest and youngest players to open.

You wouldn't exactly call what we then did a team huddle, more an embarrassed bumbling together of bodies, but we shuffled into a loose circle and wished our new season well in the time-honoured style.

'This year's about winning,' I said, and ten pairs of eyes looked back at me with the air of a vegan chef who has just learned that his new employer is Jeremy Clarkson. I knew that it would sound dumb, and it did, but it was the kind of thing that young men called Jasper in comedy glasses said in trendy management consulting firms, and that was good enough for the new me.

'OK,' I added. 'If it's not about winning, then it's about not throwing it away.'

'Attaboy!' added the Sieve cheerfully, before quickly wishing he hadn't, and heading back to his car to check if any orders had come in for his brand of industrial dishwashers.

After five overs, we were 45 for no wicket, and you didn't need to be Albert Einstein to work out that this predicted a fine total after our allotted twenty overs, possibly even as high as between 170 and 180.

We sat on a bench by the pavilion watching the action

unfold, until the Land Agent spotted my new kit.

'Look! Roger's got a new bat!' He picked it up. 'And helmet. And gloves. Did he get lucky at Christmas, or has he been practising, I wonder? You wouldn't, really, would you, Roger?'

'Don't be stupid,' I said, in the closest form of words that I could find that wasn't overtly dishonest, and I saw the Sieve grimace at my dissembling.

At that moment, a wicket fell, and suddenly it was all about me.

Me, with my new expensive bat and my new expensive helmet. Me and all that coaching, all those evenings. Me and the hip and the bruising. Me and the yoga, the X-rays and the exercising. Me with the psychologist. Me and the weight of my own expectations.

'Middle, please.'

Brian the coach had pleaded with me to change my guard from leg stump to middle, and I did as he had said. Taking a guard is to the social cricketer what carrying the *Financial Times* is to someone who works in the City: part of a defunct uniform that we still like to respect.

We used to have a poet in the team who would take a guard like the rest of us, but then seep slowly off towards the leg side, ball by ball, like lava flowing down a gentle mountainside, until he was nearer to the boundary rope than the wicket. He swore it was to be nearer his dog, who adored him.

'You have it,' said the umpire. I didn't need to glance around to see where the fielders would have been placed. Whenever I came out to bat against one of our regular oppositions, you could have sold camping rights for the evening at Cow Corner.

I rotated my right batting glove on the bat handle, and formed a 'V' that lined up with the 'V' on the back of the bat. I pushed both gloves together on the handle and gripped with sixty per cent of my power on the top hand, and forty per cent on the bottom. I held my hands in toward my chest, raised the bat towards the trees behind me, and waited for the bowler.

'Head and weight forward. Shoulder towards the ball.' The coming together of all the formal coaching and psychology in my normally free-spirited brain was creating a sense of other worldliness for me as I watched the bowler run in.

The first ball passed harmlessly to leg and was adjudged a wide by the umpire. The second was straight at the stumps and I did what I had been told to do, blocking it away with a vertical bat. Same with the third, which in days gone by would have been flayed over mid-wicket, or bowled me. And same with the fourth, the last of the over, which trickled off the edge of my bat for a single to fine leg. I felt simultaneously virtuous, for actually doing what my 'backroom staff' had been urging me to do, and an utter fraud, for daring to try to be someone I manifestly wasn't.

'Have you been practising?' asked my partner, the Accountant, as we conferred between overs.

'Why do you ask?'

'Don't know. Normally, you'd be back in the pavilion for a three-ball eight at this stage.' He looked strangely disappointed, not at all in awe of my iron discipline. We could see an old bloke with a pony tail and whiskers measuring out his run-up, and my heart lifted. I had an inkling of the genial offerings that were about to come my way, but I told the Accountant that I would watch him carefully for a ball or so and see what he did.

What he did was both interesting and arresting. What he did was bowl a ball that went twice as fast as the attendant biomechanics should have allowed it to. With gargantuan self-will, I pushed my shoulder towards its speeding form and presented the defensive, vertical bat that I had promised I would, but it made no difference. The ball was through the gate and onto the stumps before I had even transferred my weight.

I stared down at the straw-coloured wicket, up at the celebrating bowler, and then tucked my bat politely under my arm and began the long walk of shame that felt a hundred miles but was, in fact, forty or so yards. The child in me wanted to go and hide for a moment or two, and the adult was furiously trying not to add up all the pounds I had spent on getting here, and then dividing them by that one precious run in the amortisation from hell.

I met the Sieve on his way out to bat, thought of giving him some advice that would retrospectively make the bowler look more brilliant, and me less incompetent, but then thought better of it, and went back to the changing room. Quickly, the duties of captaincy filled the void that might otherwise have been occupied by gloom. I might not have had a productive innings, but I could still try as captain to influence the outcome of the match.

In a predictable age of safety and interconnectivity, heroes come in many shapes and forms. Tonight, as it turned out, the hero was the collective will of the team not to roll over and be thumped. Just as humans are often at their best with their backs to the wall, so the White Hunters are often at their best defending an inadequate score. A mixture of guilt and bloody-mindedness courses through their veins: catches actually go to hand; fielders stop balls cleanly, instead of letting them pass between their legs; and bowlers keep a semblance of control, making it tricky for the opposition batsman to score runs.

The match turned on a couple of pivotal moments, mainly courtesy of the 'youth' wing, and in particular to a single moment of genius, when one of them threw down the stumps with a direct hit from about fifty yards, and ran out their number three bat by a short head. A couple of balls later, their next man in top-edged a ball into his forehead, with similar consequences to, but much more spectacular than, my effort with the Graduate in January.

He took some time to arise from his cruciform, corpse-like state on the wicket, during which the available daylight started ebbing from the sky, therefore making it steadily more difficult for incoming players. Eventually, we ran out winners by eighteen runs.

One down, sixteen to play.

I knew the Graduate would call.

He would know from previous years that the match would finish at about 8.45 p.m., and it would take a further hour to pack up all the club kit in the car and share a cheerful beer and a sandwich with our opponents. And I knew that he might dress it all up in any way he chose, with questions about how my day had been, what my plans were for the weekend, but there was in truth only one piece of information he required from the conversation: precisely how many runs I had scored.

At 9.47 p.m., the call came.

'That's great!' he said, when I explained that we had won our opening match, and talked him through the various twists and turns. 'How did *you* get on?'

It wasn't asked competitively. It was only in my interpretation that it could possibly seem so.

'I made one.' Potential, believable excuses tumbled to the front of my mind: brilliant inswinging ball, fading light, uneven pitch, first time in a helmet, but I knew that this wasn't the year for those.

'I played down the Northern line to a good ball that was coming up the Bakerloo.' This was an old cricketing metaphor, but it told the truth more elegantly than I could.

'Are you OK with that?' This was a kindly soul second-guessing the pain of the failure.

'I am, actually. My bat was vertical and my head was down. I just played the right shot in the wrong way, simple as that.'

When I got home, there was a one-line email from Jo at the top of my inbox.

'Great to meet you today and look forward to working with you. How did you get on tonight? Kind regards, Jo.'

'I kept the faith,' I replied.

Because, under the new rules of the game, I had.

4 *College Days*

Late April

THERE is a strange connection between kick-starting a lawnmower at the beginning of the season and kick-starting a cricket team.

Both have been put back in the shed at the end of the previous September, wiped down and left to get on with it. When the lawnmower is dragged back out into the weak spring sunlight, it has got dirt in the spark plugs, its blades need a good stropping and the cylinder is shaking a little more than it was the previous summer. By some miracle of amateur engineering, it is soon firing, but doing so with an intermittent groan that suggests it will shortly be back at the garden centre, with an unfeasibly expensive bill attached to the manila label on the starter handle.

White Hunters are the same. Each spring they emerge from their houses, their farms, and their warehouses, blinking into the sunlight and wondering how it was they ever managed to bowl so much as a medium-paced ball, still less catch something hard and round, coming at them quickly, seven short months ago. Their kit bags, which were hurriedly shoved up into eleven different lofts after the last match of the season, smell faintly of damp, and are generally short of a right-handed batting glove and Velcro on the left-hand pad. The only thing that has multiplied is the number of boxes; by a mysterious osmotic process, there are now about 127 boxes associated with the club and its players, only five of which were ever purchased from real retailers in return for real money.

We are pleased to see each other, to be sure, at the first couple of games of the season, but the pleasure tends to be more gently conveyed in April than it is in September, with handshakes and polite enquiries as to well-being, rather than the hugs and abuse that are the norm later on. Like cold-blooded creatures in a zoo, we need time for the sun to warm our bones before we resemble the people we left behind last year.

The season's second game was a beer match against the staff of Churcher's College, a pleasurable hangover from the days when its professional teachers were trying to knock some sense into the Graduate and the Ginger.

Playing against staff teams from schools that take their sport seriously should carry a health warning. In reaction to the question, 'Where do retired first-class cricketers disappear to if *Test Match Special* doesn't want them?', the answer should be, 'To secondary schools, and normally the one that you are just about to play.'

The additional problem is that they are now often disguised as geography teachers, arriving at the ground in corduroy jackets with leather patches on them, and a vague academic cheerfulness associated with having just drummed into a particularly thick student that a drumlin is not a small musical instrument, but a feature of glaciation. Then you have the ex-Cambridge hockey blue, able to adapt his eye and his ball skills to any sport on earth, and when he's finished with you, the South African rugby coach, who turns out to have filled the close-season summers of his main sport by playing cricket to province level; not to mention the six-foot-eight economist, who routed us the previous year with chin-music deliveries that leapt from a good length towards our throats.

To help overcome these challenges, we had recruited three friends of the Ginger who had recently played first-team cricket for the school: a quick bowler, a leg spinner and an opening bat. In some ways it was the paradox of Theseus's Ship all over again, in that there was presumably a point at which the White Hunters had changed through the replacement of most of its original parts to something utterly different.

'Tough!' we thought. One of the basic responsibilities of sports people is to avoid humiliation, and that was all that we were doing. One of the squared circles of a social sports club is that whilst a win is always the sought-after outcome, a one-sided thrashing doesn't actually please either side. Having said that, I wouldn't know, as I'm not entirely certain we have ever thrashed anyone to that degree.

When we went out for the toss, the skipper looked quizzically at our line-up, and mentioned that he had a dim notion he had seen some of the younger members of our team before, possibly on this very pitch. As head of the Religion and Philosophy Department, he had a concerning interest in ethics that I was keen to brush off at the outset.

'Possibly,' I said. 'I just asked the boys if they had any friends around to help make up the numbers.'

'And it's lovely that all three of them happened to be in the first team here only last summer.' He tossed a pound coin up into the grey sky, and I called incorrectly.

'What would you like to do?'

This was kind, but irritating, as it put back on me the onus that I'd escaped by losing the toss, and also placed a tiresome qualification on the eventuality of a White Hunter victory.

'Not sure,' I said. 'What do you think I should do?' This was a polite version of plonking the ball back into his court, and I nodded respectfully to his own academic subject. 'What would Aristotle have done?'

He thought about this for a second. 'He once said that the aim of the wise was not to secure pleasure but to avoid pain, so I think you should bowl. If you'd asked me what Socrates would have done, I would have said bat.'

'Why?'

'Because he often explained that he is richest who is content with least. What would you like to do?'

'We'll bowl,' I said, and we agreed terms, shook hands and strolled back to the pavilion.

'Interesting toss,' I told the team. 'We lost and we are fielding. Something about Aristotle.' I suggested that the Human Sieve kept wicket for the first ten of our twenty overs, and then handed the gloves to the Beekeeper, who would have bowled his overs by then. The ill-disguised elephant trumpeting round the room was that the only two people in the team who didn't already know that the Sieve was the worst wicket-keeper in the world were our new strike bowler, who had recently been clocked in a county trial at eighty-two miles per hour, and our new leg spinner.

To them, the Sieve was in all probability a crafty old veteran of bygone varsity matches, someone who had gradually replaced the vigour of his youth with the guile of a sporting Machiavelli. To the Sieve, on the other hand, leg spin was another country where they did things differently. Very differently. The last time he had seen leg spin was when Abdul Qadir ran through the England line-up at the Oval in 1987, when he was an inebriated spectator. The concept of its direct intersection with his life was an entirely unfamiliar one, and he had never given the matter so much as a moment's thought.

'You know he's a leggie, don't you?' the Tree Hugger asked him, whilst pointing out the new bowler.

'I'm very happy for him,' came the reply.

I gave the young fast bowler the opening over, as much because 'quicks' get sad if they don't bowl with shine on the ball as for any tactical reason, and I stood with him as he set his own field. It's a funny old thing about 'proper' bowlers: some don't want anything to do with the field placing, as if consideration of such trifles insults their lofty expertise; others fiddle around endlessly ball by ball, making alterations that are so sub-atomically small, it would need a micrometer to work out what had actually changed. My new quick fell into the latter category.

'On the one for me, please,' he said to the Wealth Manager, who hadn't got the faintest clue what he was on about, and started his long, habitual pilgrimage to the depths of long on, where he could dream contentedly about the arrival of a crate of Montepulciano *de Ricci*, which was due at his house in the next day or so.

'On the forty-five for me, please,' he called out to the Breeder down at fine leg, getting his head round the next over that he would be bowling. The Breeder smiled genially and stayed exactly where he was.

'Fly slip, please,' he said to the Ginger. This was a problem, as I had quietly agreed with the Ginger that he should go to long stop, down on the boundary immediately behind the wicket-keeper. It is not a position you see often, or ever, in first-class cricket, but it is one that you see all the time with the White Hunters, when anyone is bowling at over forty miles per hour, and the Sieve is keeping. It turns a certain four runs into one, time after time, and is often the most effective position in the entire field.

The Ginger looked at me for advice, and I made a signal designed to convey the impression that he should stay where the bowler had put him for the time being, and then walk briskly to long stop while the bowler was walking back to his mark, and therefore wouldn't be looking. After all, we were still at the stage of persuading our guest players that we were skilled practitioners of the game.

'Play,' said the umpire.

The fast bowler, whose run-up apparently started somewhere near the leisure centre a mile to the south, sprinted in with the magnificent smoothness of a blond Malcolm Marshall, and unleashed a ferocious outswinger, of a sort that frankly we don't see too often at our level of cricket. Knowing that, even in a Twenty20 match, discretion is sometimes the better part of valour, the batsman removed his bat and gloves from harm's way and let it through to the keeper.

The keeper, for his part, had never seen anything moving that quickly or scarily in his life, at least not since he had been stopped for speeding outside Bridport. Respectfully, he also removed his own gloves from harm's way, waving the ball on its way down to the still untenanted position of long stop, where it lodged itself under a rhododendron shrub. The umpire signalled four byes, and the Sieve muttered something about 'not being quite ready', and apologised to the bowler.

A man can only use the 'wasn't quite ready' excuse credibly once, and by the time the second ball was bowled, the Sieve was standing another ten yards back, and the bowler had accepted that an additional long stop was probably a good option. The fifth ball was a pre-arranged short one, pre-arranged in the sense that the bowler had given a signal to the Sieve, who, in turn, didn't quite have the necessary confidence to ask what it meant. In the event, it didn't matter. The batsman took it on, and swung his bat through an arc in front of his chest before top-edging it mightily up in the air, high above mid on, who safely caught it on the first attempt. Reader, I was that mid on, and that catch temporarily changed everything for the better.

The next three or four overs went as well as we could have hoped. Churcher's had their best batsmen in, which meant that little or nothing got left for the wicket-keeper, and the two opening bowlers kept things nice and quiet, until a couple of boundaries persuaded me that we needed a spell from our leg spinner. Suddenly, I felt very grown up.

In thirty years, I had never captained a really competitive leg spinner, and for a moment or two, it gave me a sense of mastery over the opposition. After all, they had trained him in his early days, and they would be only too aware of how he had developed in the intervening years. However, if anything, they looked rather unconcerned, and the spinner himself was emphatically casual in the matter of field placing before he bowled his first ball.

'Shove them where you fancy,' he told me. Somehow, I

imagined that the great Anil Kumble wouldn't necessarily have told Rahul Dravid to 'shove them where he fancied', and that, if he had, the Indian captain might have had something to say about it, but I let it pass. Six balls later, I began dimly to understand his lack of interest.

He had recently completed a gap year, whose prime ingredient seemed to have been an itinerary through every available Class A narcotic in South-East Asia, as well as each Full Moon Party in Thailand, and finally the contents of every bar and pub in the area since he had returned. He may once have been a budding leg-spin bowler, but for the time being, he was a man with about as much control on his moving parts as the collapsing chimney of a power station, and the muse had well and truly left him.

It would not be for me to guess what he was trying to achieve with each ball, but the resulting over was painful in its variances, and its cost. By the end of it, even the Sieve looked like a proper cricketer.

'Take a break,' I said, as kindly as a man can, when thirty-three per cent of his grand plan has turned to ashes in front of him.

'Thanks,' he said. 'I wasn't getting much purchase off the grass.' Possibly not, but 'purchase' and 'grass', I surmised, were concepts that regretfully he had left behind in Koh Phangan, and they had certainly not played any part in the last few minutes of play.

The curse of the self-appointed ringer had struck once again.

At the end of their twenty overs, the school staff had amassed 140 runs, in part due to some uncomplicated hitting from that rugby-teaching son of the high veldt. It was a steep total, but not an unreachable one, provided we didn't lose our heads, and knocked them off at the rate of seven runs an over. Sometimes these things look laughably easy, until they don't. For the time being, we didn't know for which side of the divide we were destined.

In a nod to whatever excellence I felt I had temporary access, I asked last year's school first XI opener to do the same honours for us, and I gave him the Graduate as his partner, partly as a familiar face, but mainly as a homicidal stroke-maker, whose brutality came off on our behalf enough times for it to be worth a try.

It is a good idea to return to your *alma mater* from time to time, if only for the sense that, whether they choose to admit it or not, logic suggests they have had a hand in whatever might have gone visibly wrong with your life. In this case, it was in the matter of dress and equipment. Due to an administrative confusion between the Tree Hugger and me, fifty per cent of our club kit was in a barn somewhere near West Meon, and none of the five younger players appeared to have registered that this was a cricket match, traditionally played in whites, as opposed to a kick around in the local park.

Certain logistical phenomena happen frequently enough to be set down:

1. The scorebook can be relied upon to be on the kitchen sideboard of whichever of us isn't playing in the current match.

2. One of the two kit bags, on the other hand, can be relied upon to be in whichever of the Tree Hugger's pick-up trucks his assistant has driven down to Fordingbridge to

deliver a late season order of 1,500 mixed native farm hedging plants.

3. Whichever bag makes it to the match will have all the bats in it, and none of the pads, or vice-versa. Plus a couple of squashed Cadbury's mini-rolls that the Tree Hugger spirited into the bag for the long drive back to Winchester, and had then forgotten.

4. A brand-new match ball behaves less impressively once the resident Jack Russell has found it and decided that it is a strange rodent that needs killing.

5. When it is sunny, everyone simultaneously forgets their caps.

6. It is only when it is cold, and when sweaters are donned for the first time, that many White Hunters get the dawning realisation that they have gone up a size during the winter.

7. Every day is dress-down Friday for the Ginger, whilst the Gun Runner still loudly bemoans the passing of flannel trousers, long-sleeved cricket shirts and the age of deference.

8. No one ever remembers to switch on the tea urn. (*See also Chapter Eight: The desiderata of social cricket captaincy.*)

9. When the tea urn is eventually switched on, no one ever remembers to switch it back off again.

10. The only way to guarantee a decent tea, when players are bringing component parts of it themselves, is by directly connecting positions in the batting order with the quality of the offering. Flaccid Tesco Value sandwiches are suddenly replaced by home-made, four-layered organic cakes that would not be disgraced in *The Great British Bake Off* grand final.

Finally, we had found enough kit for the Graduate and the star batsman to go out into the middle and face the music. To our surprise, the former took the first ball, and then played no less than three exquisitely elegant forward-defensive practice shots before bunting the delivery eighty-five yards and halfway across an adjacent rugby pitch.

There is a well-concealed elegance to the Graduate's play; everything he does immediately before and after the ball is delivered is technically perfect, redolent of a Tendulkar or a Root. It is only during the single second of the ball itself that the underlying sport changes to golf: out comes the nine iron and then the violent heave somewhere between mid-wicket and long on is brought into play.

It has served him well over many years, and it is only jeopardised by his determination on occasions to reprise something he saw Jos Buttler do on a YouTube clip, or when he is simply trying to stay in, rather than score runs. Whatever else the Graduate was put on earth to do, it was not occupation of the crease.

Thus, in their contrasting styles, the two openers flayed the bowling to all parts, until they had both reached twenty-five and consequently had to be retired. Even then the merriment continued: the Tree Hugger, who had clearly learned more than me at our covert net sessions, batted with a rare assurance; and had it not been for his attempting an injudicious run with a player a third of his age, who lapped him halfway down the home straight, he would probably have needed to be retired, too.

We were 80 for one after eight overs, and with only sixty-one to get in the last twelve and nine wickets in hand, it was mere child's play; possibly the widest open goal we would have before us all season. Had we not spent a third of a century preparing ourselves for moments such as these, for the calm procession to victory that an assured all-round performance suggests?

Apparently not, and possibly for two reasons. The first and lesser reason was that the religion and philosophy skipper suddenly remembered that he had a South African provincial player, and an ex-first-class geography-teaching bowler, who had turned out for Essex a few times in his heyday until, like everyone else, he had fallen out with Graham Gooch. But the real cause of what happened next could be called poverty of ambition.

The problem that has dogged us ever since the club was formed, back when America was an unknown land across the western horizon, is that we turn out to be easily scared by heights, and the higher we go, the more easily we are scared. Then the more scared we become, the more we do something stupid.

On came Essex man and the South African, and through the crease came a succession of White Hunters, impermanence writ large across their faces and through their body language.

'We only need five an over,' called the Tree Hugger forlornly to no one in particular, as they headed out to the middle to replace an outgoing batsman. 'Give yourself a chance. Play yourself in.'

And one by one we went out there, and one by one we came back. The Breeder, chopping a ball onto his stumps that would have been called a wide even if the umpire was a resident of the Royal School for the Blind; the Ginger, lofting a full ball vertically up into the gathering gloom, and having enough time to complete two comfortable runs before it came to rest in the bowler's outstretched hands; and the Sieve, swishing at a nothing ball that went on to swish at his stumps.

'Moved in the air, and off the seam,' he announced to the bemused spectators, as he made his way back to the pavilion. 'Or I did. One or the other.'

Not for the last time in the season, it was left to the Beekeeper and me to get us across the line. We were eight wickets down, with only the catatonic leg spinner to come after us. As I walked out to join him, I reassured the Beekeeper that I was fresh from more cricketing nets than I had ever had in my life, and I was confident that we could make it. Time and overs were not the issue. No, the issue was lying on the ground seventy yards away, smoking a roll-up and watching the blue smoke rise up into the chestnut leaves above. He was all that stood between us and defeat if one of us now got out.

'Put me in at eleven,' he had said, when I was writing down the batting order. 'I haven't got my contact lenses in this evening, and I can't bat for shit even when I can see things properly.' As a personal statement of intent, it was pretty unequivocal.

I arrived at the crease and the skipper came out to meet me on my way in.

'Do you know that Matthew Hayden once said that he had seen God, and that he batted number four for India? We expect no less from you.' Then, as an afterthought he added reflectively, 'Wittgenstein was a keen cricket supporter as well, you know, in his Cambridge days.'

In the complex intersections between philosophy and cricket, between his career and his pleasure, I had to admit that the man had it all covered.

All I had to do now was what Brian the coach had told me to do back at Arundel all those weeks ago. Point the left shoulder at the ball, and watch the ball all the way onto the bat. 'V of the hand opposite the V on the back of the bat,' I told myself. Hands to the chest. Bat out behind, slightly above the horizontal. Be a good coach to myself.

It was only while the bowler was preparing to deliver the first ball I was to face that I realised something was going horribly wrong: my brain couldn't get the mantra of coaching out of itself, and was now permanently chanting like a salutation to the community of noble disciples in a Buddhist shrine. It wouldn't shut up, and I couldn't make it.

Hands to the chest, it said, as the bowler got to the top of his run-up. *Shoulder to the ball. Vertical bat.*

'Shut up!' I hissed.

Om mani padme hum, it might as well have been saying, as he ran in to deliver the ball.

Maintain the V. Be peaceful. Shoulder to the ball. Metta Sutta.

'Shut the fuck up!' I cried, as the ball bore down on me.

In that instant, my brain broke free and muscle memory took over. It was a short ball and I swung through, made good connection, and sent it steepling over the top of square leg and on its way to the new swimming pool that the high sheriff of Hampshire had been pleased to declare open only a couple of weeks before.

The Beekeeper wandered down the pitch, prodding aimlessly at things as a signal that he wouldn't mind a chat.

'Was that your coaching, then?' he asked. 'If I didn't know any better, I would have said that was what you've been doing for the last two hundred matches.'

'Just before that shot,' said the keeper, when I got back to my crease. 'Did you just say what I think you said?' I admitted that I had and explained what was going on in the porridge that passed as my brain.

'No worries,' he said. 'Only, normally it's the keeper who sledges the batsman, and I got a bit confused there.'

Who knows what might have happened had the adult been resident in my head, rather than the attention-deficit child from the institution? I determined that, whatever the South African bowled at me next ball, I would come down and meet it respectfully with the full, defensive face of my bat. When he bowled what turned out to be a leg-stump long hop that should have been flayed to the swimming pool or beyond, I took a step forward with my left foot, and patted it defensively straight into the hands of the nearby short leg fielder, who gratefully pouched it.

It was only the second time that I had ever got out to a defensive shot, and for a while I felt that the shame would do me in. Back in 1995, I remembered as I trudged back to the pavilion, Alan Wells had done the same thing to his very first ball, a long hop from Curtly Ambrose in the former's one and only match for England. Wells was Sussex skipper at the time, and we supporters were thrilled that one of our own had finally got the call at the age of thirty-four, and we hoped that he would carry his sensational form into the Test arena. The occasion had got to him in front of 18,000 spectators at the Oval, and he had simply played the wrong shot.

The same had happened to me here, of course, only in front of nine mystified teammates and a Gordon Setter that had strayed on to the pitch to empty its bowels at deep extra cover a few moments before.

'Nice one, Rog,' called out the Beekeeper cheerfully, now stranded with his myopic, half-stoned partner. 'Was that the coaching?'

Twenty minutes later, we were drinking beer and eating school sandwiches, our fifteen-run defeat intellectualised into being the result of a slight imbalance between the teams. Rain, which had been threatening all evening, started to come down in earnest, and I had that old familiar joy that only a cricketer knows, when the weather intervenes shortly after the match is done and dusted and the kit is back in the car.

Conversation had swiftly moved on from our defeat to the kind of stuff that bonds teams together who have the good fortune to operate on the same wavelength.

'Have you had lessons, by any chance?' asked the school's skipper.

'Certainly not!' I laughed. 'That would be the sign of desperation, even for me.' The lie fell easily from my lips, as a handful of lessons would have been justifiable only with a much more compelling performance than mine.

'I thought not,' he replied. 'It's just that someone said you had. Don't worry, though, we could see in an instant that they were misled.'

He winked at me, and then got out his diary to pencil in our next fixture for the equivalent day the following year.

5 Metamorphosis

May

SUNSHINE had stolen away the memory of the long winter.

One morning, it just happened. It was as if I was pushing my way back through the hanging fur coats and tumbling out of the Narnian cupboard and into the bedroom, away from the snowy trees, the icy castle, the fauns and the half-light.

Where there had been only recently swollen rivers, puddles, potholes, greyness and damp piles of last autumn's rotting leaves, now there was almost more light than I knew what to do with. The kind of light that begins before five in the morning, streaming through the gaps in the bedroom curtains and forming spotlit cones of moving dust particles above the old sofa, like some scene in a theatre. Light that reflects back up from the woods and fields in the valley below in any shade of green that any artist in history has ever confected, and then a few more. Light that brings heat in its wake, that activates the smells and sounds of early summer – the blossom of the mock orange, or the snap of an old blue Provençal tablecloth being shaken free of the crumbs from the first outside lunch of the year.

These were the days when the centre of gravity of our settled lives began to shift from indoors to outdoors, and where the ways in which we filled our time had less to do with our minds than our bodies. Out of the cupboards gradually tumbled the tools of summer: tennis rackets, sunglasses, croquet mallets, baseball caps, old packets of vegetable seeds, firelighters and cricket stumps. Sandpaper and teak oil were applied to the ageing garden furniture in the optimistic belief that this would see them through one more season.

Renewal is the word of the moment. Out with the old, in with the new. This summer must count, as never before.

IT is the time when cricket is at her most beguiling, and most subversive.

For a start, she is everywhere: on the advertising hoardings in the Jubilee Line stations, and displayed in the front windows of bookshops; on the village greens seen from high up on an evening railway embankment, and down at the county ground. She has been hidden in football's shadow these last seven months, adrift in a world of someone else's news, and now she is politely coughing for our attention. Politicians use her in their metaphors more than ever in the late spring, with their talk of 'getting onto the front foot', 'holding an end up' and of being plain 'stumped'. Someone writes an article about the slow death of the game, just as three quarters of a million of us reach up into the loft to bring out our kit and breathe new life into it all.

New life. That is what all this should be about, and what it *would* be about, were it not for that uninvited, unwelcome elephant chuntering away in the corner of the room. If you run an internet search on 'mid-life crisis', you will find that it is an all-encompassing term for that fifteen-year period spent getting used to getting old. It is the self-doubt that creeps in when either you, or your body, wake up one morning to discover that there is less life ahead of you than behind you, and it falls into an orderly panic. So orderly, that only you notice it at first.

In my own case, the mid-life crisis rather lacked the magnificence that I had always planned for it. Rather than heading off to buy a few grams of Red Lebanese from a dodgy dealer in Marrakesh, or hurtling into an Indian sunset on a throbbing Ducati, my own quiet revolution involved becoming mildly irritable, doing crosswords and making lists. Endless reams of lists. Lists about things so inconsequential as to have never been listed before. And spending hours doing nothing. And more hours actually planning what nothing I might do next.

If a psychologist ever asked me how this condition had presented in me, this is how I might have described a typical evening on my own:

18.45:   My wife Caroline goes to art class. I have approximately four hours to achieve things or paint the town blue. I make a cup of tea.

19.04:   Listen to *The Archers*, even though it has driven me mad for nearly forty years.

19.16:   Make a list of the things I want to achieve during the evening.

19.35:   Wash up supper. Realise with sense of injustice that this wasn't on the list in the first place, and therefore doesn't constitute a bankable achievement. Write it on the list, and then cross it out with a different coloured pen.

19.40:   See dog lying on back with paws in the air. Take cute picture. Post on Facebook.

19.45:   Turn on Facebook to see if anyone has liked post. They haven't. Notice post about high achieving friend's daughter's pony club victory. Refuse to like it out of pure spite.

19.55:   Channel hop to see if any cricket is on. Watch three episodes of *Family Guy* when it isn't.

20.25:   Think of wonderful first line for new poem and write it down, without first having any idea of what poem might actually be about. Find artistic virtue in screwing up paper seeing if I can throw it into the wickerwork recycling bin from across the room.

20.26:   Dog retrieves bit of paper and brings it back, thinking this is the start of some entertaining game.

20.30:   Go back to list and cross out something gratuitously.

20.40:   Read two pages of newspaper and decide to update life list of birds.

21.42:   Pour glass of wine and get nostalgic. Delete Facebook post as still without a like.

21.44: Watch YouTube video of Ben Stokes's 258 at Cape Town in 2016. Then watch Brian Lara's match-winning 153 against the Australians in 1999.

22.16: Hear car in drive. Look busy. Put kettle back on again.

22.42: Put list in bin.

22.44: Write email to players for Saturday's match at Arundel, confirming details.

It wasn't like this all the time, of course, but in a very real sense, my get up and go had got up and gone, and, like an old friendship where the two of you have fallen out, I wanted it back.

IT had taken us over a decade of effort to secure the invitation to ply our trade at the Castle Ground at Arundel, possibly the most beguiling setting for cricket in England, and certainly the only one that afforded people like us the opportunity to play on a first-class venue. From being a process that made acquiring hens' teeth look simple, recruitment for the team was, just this once, laughably easy. Almost every person on our mailing list of seventy suddenly seemed to forget how busy they were in their garden, how much they needed to collect Child A from university, or attend Niece B's confirmation, or how that irritating hamstring niggle prevented them from helping us out – and they all volunteered.

Anyone who runs a social cricket side will be familiar with the Friday evening ring-round to anyone they know in possession of two eyes and a functioning pulse in a last-ditch attempt to make up the numbers for Saturday's match. The process is known to Richard and me as *Operation Wake the Dead*. Like a rural version of the a three-line whipped vote in the House of Commons, we have been known to ambush people coming home from hospital for a long recuperation, purely so that we can have an eleventh, albeit pallid, immobile and miserable, player.

Players who hadn't answered an email in years, let alone turned out for us, were mysteriously back in the fold, signing off their emails with sentiments expressing how wonderful we both were to be still organising these things after thirty years, and how they couldn't wait to see us at Arundel. When all was said and done, we had over forty-five volunteers for the eleven places, which was approximately nine times the amount we normally got on the first mail-out.

So we contrived what, in hindsight, must have been the most cack-handed, unfair and mysterious selection system in the history of the sport, in an effort to whittle the forty-five down to eleven. In so doing, we managed to cause more offence and confusion than Kevin Pietersen's entire England career.

We created a set of opaque criteria that was originally designed to deliver eleven relatively competent, committed and genial people to the ground. The arcane recipe included length of time with the club, commitment to matches, ability to bat, bowl or field spectacularly, and other factors now thankfully lost in the mists of time. We then had to allow for the Tree Hugger and me, who probably wouldn't have made the cut if we had adhered to the strict criteria, which meant we were only looking for nine.

We then we auctioned off two spaces to raise cash for a cause close to our hearts, which meant we needed only seven. One of these places was snapped up for £200 by the scion of a noble banking family, who had never played for us before, and for whom this was loose change; the other going to me for £150, so that I could ensure that at least one of my children would get the treat.

The Human Sieve, who had longed to play at Arundel for an eternity, missed the cut and very nearly decided never to play for us again. Only the Ginger came out of this with any credit, surrendering his possible place on the basis that he felt he hadn't been committed enough to the team this season to merit it. At the end of it all, we had our eleven, but the process of getting there had been more complex than building a medium-sized aircraft carrier, and as divisive as a presidential tweet.

All that was left now was to count down the days, and to check the BBC ten-day weather map for Brighton every seven or eight minutes to make sure God wasn't about to intervene in some dumb meteorological way.

Most matches, we struggle to get a full team to the ground in time for a prompt start, but not at Arundel. The resident tawny owls hadn't even completed their night's work by the time the first White Hunter turned up, almost as if the ground would disappear, or be let to someone else, if he didn't guard it. Three hours before the match, most of us were there, walking our dogs around the outfield, taking selfies, and laying out sumptuous picnics that belied the limp Tesco ham-and-tomato sandwich that was our normal fare.

Our younger players were camping out in the indoor nets with the bowling machine, and inventing shots of exquisite excellence that were fated never to see the light of day out in the middle. In anticipation of the coming match, the Graduate had put in about fifteen hours of practice in the nets and our garden the previous weekend, and five times that amount in his head.

Over breakfast, lunch and tea, he had told us and anyone

else who would listen how it was going to be, how to deal with the big boundaries, and how to keep our heads when all around were losing theirs. To say that he was up for it would have been a hideous under-exaggeration: it was manifesting itself within him like a vast, urban construction project.

'Where would you like me to bat, skipper?' asked the scion of the banking dynasty, as I was packing away our lunch.

Every captain knows that this is not the innocent request it seems. For a start, it absolutely precludes the answer 'eleven' or 'ten', openly defies the answer 'nine' or 'eight', and would rather avoid the answer 'one' or 'two'. All it wants is to hear any number between 'three' and 'seven' which, given that Richard and I will probably occupy two of those positions, ultimately means that only around a quarter of supplicants are going to be happy. You get used to it.

In an improvement on Churcher's College the week before, I won the toss and asked the opposition to bat. This was mainly because doing the match in this order at least guaranteed that we would be playing for thirty-five overs, plus however many balls it took to get rid of us. I mentioned that we traditionally played a 'not out first ball' rule, so that a batsman who had driven eighty miles for the game could at least have a cost-free yahoo when he got to the crease, but my opposite number felt that he could probably live without it, and I lacked the courage to press my case.

Back in the day, the first match for every touring team in England would be a one-day affair against the Duchess of Norfolk's XI on this ground, a team made up out of England hopefuls, and Sussex seconds. So now I could emulate the sight I had seen so often of captains like Allan Border, Brian Lara and Sachin Tendulkar leading their sides into the field down the steps from the pavilion with that sprightly step, and those pristine whites. And that was roughly where the brush with excellence stopped.

We didn't bowl or field badly, and after twenty-five of their allotted thirty-five overs, we had restricted them to a very manageable number of runs. Even after the last ten, where our bowling had been taken to with alarming enthusiasm by their middle order batsmen, we were still only faced with a chase that was a fraction under a run a ball. To be honest, we rather fancied it, and I prepared a batting order that for once reflected the needs of the team, rather than the evidence of how successfully the various batsmen within it had privately negotiated with me.

We would open with the Merchant Banker (after all, £200 is £200), and with the Tree Hugger, with his newly acquired excellence, courtesy of Brian the coach a month or so ago in the indoor nets of this very ground. The rest of us settled on the warm, sunny bank to watch our reply begin, imagining the crowd, and noting with interest the four slips lining up in an arc to the right of the wicket-keeper.

Ball one was a disappointment, in that the banking heir did the cricketing version of throwing someone's entire portfolio on some dodgy Russian gas stock, drove sumptuously at the new ball, and carted it onto his stumps via a thick inside edge. Nought for one. He walked back to muted applause, it being slightly ironic to celebrate the performance of a man who has paid £200 for the privilege of spending five seconds doing something painfully incompetent, and patently unsuccessful.

Ball two was not much better. The incoming batsman, the Beekeeper, came forward in a hideous parody of contrived defence, and softly patted a catch back to the bowler, who duly and gratefully pouched it. Nought for two. At this point, the Wealth Manager was the next batsman due in. He had been reading the *Sunday Times* sports section in the sunshine, and planned on a relaxing half hour or so of doing the same. Now he couldn't find any left-hand pads and was running around like a Tasmanian Devil, swearing at his dog as a substitute for doing anything practical about it. Finally, he came out to face the hat-trick ball.

In comparison to balls one and two, ball three was a complete triumph. The Wealth Manager, having found his pads, but still livid with his dog in a textbook exhibition of borderline personality disorder, flayed the ball angrily over the slip cordon and watched it run away to the third man boundary. It seemed to settle him down, and he saw out balls four, five and six in a more traditional and fitting style.

The Tree Hugger had been waiting for the next moment for half a century. He had been watching the action unfold up the other end and hadn't yet faced a ball. Now it was his turn; not only to ply his new-found excellence on one of the most exquisite settings in the country, but to be the anchor point onto which the rest of the team could cling. Every cricketing moment he had lived through in the last fifty years was in some way a preparation for this one. He waved his bat around a bit in a manner calculated to denote authority and competence, and then waited for his first ball.

As it happens, he waited rather too long, for the ball was through him and onto his stumps before he had time to blink. Four for three. He maintained the final position of his forward defensive stroke for a few seconds, as if to make the point to the watching world that he hadn't perished rashly, and he had tried to do the right thing. His walk back to the pavilion was almost too painful for his friends to watch, and we let him grieve alone under the spreading chestnut tree with the safety of distance, and in the dignity of silence.

The team situation was now circling the plughole. Hours

ago, we had hoped for a close game, even a victory. Then we had looked at the opposition total between innings and thought that a hard-fought draw might be a realistic assessment of our abilities; these were proper club bowlers, and they wouldn't be dishing out the help-yourself offerings that we would get every five or six balls from the kinds of team we normally played.

At nought for two, we had reduced our ambitions to some kind of plucky rearguard action and possibly heroic defeat with a couple of overs to go. But we were now quickly getting to the point where a total in double figures would be a relief. The gorgeousness of the surroundings was suddenly in stark contrast to the hideousness of our predicament. However, cometh the hour, cometh the man.

The Tree Hugger's denouement brought the Graduate to the wicket. Like the previous batsman, he had been ready for hours, years even, and he may well have slept in his pads the night before. Before the Tree Hugger was off the field, the Graduate was striding out, bristling with intent and purpose; greeting the opposition fielders like old friends, and telling his fellow batsman in a short mid-wicket conference how this mess was going to be sorted, and how it was going to be. He asked the umpire for a middle and leg guard, and then surveyed the fielders. The bowler went back to his mark, and made a couple of last minute adjustments to the protective ring around the batsman.

Times such as these are not relaxing ones for a parent, doubly not so if the parent is also captain. Birds may well have been singing their hearts out on the sylvan fringes of the ground, but I was living minute by minute through the various scenarios that might unfold, and seeing potential disaster wherever I looked.

Wanting the best for your children is as natural as apple pie; not understanding when you no longer have the power to affect it, on the other hand, isn't.

What everyone else saw was a cheerful twenty-three-year-old striding to the crease to have a bit of a swing in a social cricket match; what I saw was a function of the hopes and fears that I knew were tied up in the coming minutes, and the prospect of failure wasn't entirely straightforward.

The next ball, the eighth of the innings, was, in hindsight, the one with the outcome easiest to predict. I am sure that when it left the bowler's hand twenty-two yards to the east of him, the Graduate had every intention of playing the appropriate shot to whatever came his way. But that's not the point. Let's say that it takes around half a second for a ball to travel the length of a pitch when it is bowled at around seventy miles per hour. Half a second is a light year among the synapses of the human brain, and is time enough to decide many consecutive, and possibly mutually incompatible, things.

It didn't help that the Graduate's set-up position to receive a ball looked less like the prelude to a cultured cricket shot, and more like the action in a seventeenth-century Irish skirmish, where someone was about to be taken out by a shillelagh. It didn't help that there were close fielders both behind and in front of the bat, and that the Graduate is the kind of player who inevitably attracts some chirp from them, and returns it in spades. It didn't help that the Wealth Manager had met him as he was coming in and advised him to 'play his natural game'. It didn't even help that his mother, who limits her attendance at cricket matches to a strict one a year, had chosen today to come along and watch her little darling smite the ball to all parts. After all, that was distinctly what he had told her at breakfast he was going to do.

All of which probably goes some way to explaining why the Graduate ultimately decided to try to put a straightish ball into the River Arun a few hundred yards to the east, missed it by a mile, and heard the stumps rearranging themselves in a violent act of feng shui behind him. Four for four. He never looked behind him; he never glanced up at the celebrating players. He just tucked his bat politely under his arm and walked back to the pavilion.

I now had three simultaneous crises going on, each requiring a different set of solutions. I was captain of a team that was in a state of embarrassing implosion, father of a child in a state of mourning and, critically, I myself was the next man in but one. I was also the temporary scorer and incidentally trying urgently to track down batsman number eight, who had headed off for an hour's shopping in Arundel with his wife, in the expectation that his services wouldn't be needed for at least an hour. I thought briefly of why we all play sport, and in particular of Marty Rubin's assertion that 'leisure isn't always relaxation, but it's relaxation that counts'. If only.

I went to the changing room to pad up, and found the Graduate, head in hands, staring down at the floor.

'Don't tell me what I did,' he said. 'I *know* what I bloody well did. It's because I'm an idiot. A drag anchor on the team. Just can't cope with it.'

I was about to say something to him when the Young Farmer walked in. He was number nine, but had clocked that number eight was still in retail therapy some distance away, and worked out that he had better prepare himself to go out. He caught my eye in a way that suggested that what the Graduate needed right now was a friend, not a parent. And anyway, I heard the assertive cheer of a fielding side that have taken yet another wicket, and it was time for me to be the sacrificial lamb.

Eighteen for five. (Our lowest ever score was 32, which was still very much in play at this stage.)

In the end we made it to around 130, a respectable score, but still seventy short of theirs. My own contribution was fifteen scratchy runs, at least half of which were from the edge of the bat rather than the middle. Still I kept the faith and presented a tedious, vertical bat to the oncoming balls. Others cashed in on the offerings of more part-time bowlers, and we shook hands as we walked back up the bank to drink beer in the May evening sunshine.

The Graduate was with the rest of our younger players, ragging around and drawing from bottles of now warm lager. Quietly, I thanked the Young Farmer for helping him back on the rails.

'Back on the rails?' he said. 'He just needed a quiet few minutes, like we all do. And probably half an hour away from his family.' And I knew what he meant. 'Family' was a polite way of saying 'father'.

THE following day, I was back on the psychologist's couch for my second session. Jo asked me how I distinguished internally between my different roles in the team.

'What point do you focus on yourself as a player, rather than you as captain?'

It was a good question. I admitted that my preparation for batting at Arundel had been sub-optimal, to say the least, and she suggested that in future I found some quiet time to get into whatever zone my body would allow me. Going out there with a clear head was a bit of a prerequisite to doing the best I could.

'What's important to you in cricket?' she asked suddenly. 'What are the values that keep bringing you back to the game? These are things that it will be useful for you to know.'

And from there, it was a short loop to work our way back to the endless 'captain's picks' at school, those break times where it was fated to be between me and the lanky boy with the broken NHS glasses as to who would be the last man standing alone, the only one who had not been selected. That indirectly made the identification of values all those years later laughably easy.

'Friendship, belonging and status.' Call them values, or call them whatever you want; it was those that kept me coming back year after year. Then I added: 'You could throw in empathy, as well, I think. Both ways.'

For many reasons, cricket sustains empathy more than almost any other sport apart from, possibly, golf. There are few venues more public on which to display your own individual fragility than a cricket ground, and no better place to do your bit to make the world a better place by not sticking the boot in.

I explained that, whilst trying not to labour the cliché, cricket to me was a low-cost opportunity to live and relive some of life's relationships and challenges in miniature. Hopes, fears, ambitions and regrets all queued up to be dealt with as the game progressed, and the trick was not to let any one of them assert itself more than it should once real life is resumed.

'I get the feeling that you think you've treated the game right, and the game has rewarded you for it.' She was correct. I did. And it had, tenfold.

'But ultimately, it's still possibly about you proving yourself. And for this to work, you are probably going to have to work out to whom you're trying to prove it.'

I climbed back in the car after the session was over, and slowly arrived at the conclusion that what I had embarked on was a circular journey during which I was fated to meet a slightly annoying, younger version of myself coming round each and every corner, and asserting his right to be remembered. Because the uncomfortable truth was that I could only ever be a sum of all the things that had happened to me, and that I had done.

And I needed to be at peace with that idea.

And have a beer.

6 Beauty and the Sieve

June

ONE day in early June, high summer and Ginger came eastwards up the A303 alongside each other, the former with humid sunshine and thunderstorms, and the latter with piles of unwashed clothes and books about philosophy.

The Ginger's attitude to sport in general, and cricket in particular, is very different to his brother's, in that sport for him is generally an extension of his social life conducted in agreeable surroundings, with the actual result only truly relevant to pedants. Nevertheless, he has become steadily more committed to the club, and would go on to star in our breathless three-wicket victory over Alstonefield, in our Staffordshire tour a few months later.

Like the Sieve, he possesses only two shots, a pull and a thumping lofted drive, but unlike the Sieve, he generally makes contact. His round-arm bowling has an air of 'Slinga' Malinga about it, or would have if Malinga had long ginger hair and about thirty miles an hour less pace.

Last time he was at home, I had been on the point of giving up the whole thing, so he was intrigued when I told him enthusiastically about the season, about our three losses and one victory, only narrowly avoiding mentioning the coaching, the new kit and the psychologist's couch.

The Ginger loves cricket mainly for its aesthetics. Many are the times a ball has sauntered past him at deep long on, only to find that he has been staring at the beauty of a cloud formation above second slip, and has missed its presence entirely. The opportunities to be a spectator in the ongoing natural drama of the various ecosystems around an English cricket pitch sometimes, maybe even often, outweigh for him the pursuit of that most bourgeois of concepts, the victory. Stripped to its bare essentials, cricket for Al amounts to the physical wing of a diverse and intense social life, and the unspoken deal is that it is never allowed to crowd it out, or to inconvenience it.

'So, you're enjoying it again?' he asked, as we neared the end of our journey home. 'How's the batting?'

I agreed that I was much more relaxed about it this season, and that, while the batting hadn't truly fired up yet, I felt rather more in control of it than previously. He seemed relieved, so I told him about all the others, and asked whether he was free to play the coming weekend in Dorset. As is the way with undergraduates, and how their summers unfold, you have to grab them while you can. Bogota or Boomtown will have them, if you don't.

'I'd love to,' he said.

THE forthcoming Sunday match featured the longest-standing of our remaining oppositions, the Hammer Bottoms.

Over the years, many oppositions had ebbed out of the estuary of our lives, borne away by the tidal forces of diverging standards and ambitions as often as not, only to be replaced by others coming in on the next flood, surrounded by the refreshed surroundings of newness and anticipation. But the Bottoms, as they liked to be known, hung on in there season after season, based on mutual affection, and a curious interest in what exactly we had all become as one year succeeded the next.

As the years passed, we grew older together, watching our children grow, discussing our aches and pains, and even participating in each other's tragedies. When our spinner, the Yacht Designer, died, the Bottoms sent a deputation to the memorial service as if we were one of the royal houses of Europe, which was one of the reasons we loved them.

The only way in which we really differed from each other was in the off season, when their slightly less-stringent financial limitations sent them off to tours of India, Singapore, Thailand and all points in-between. Suddenly, our tours of Derbyshire and the Cotswolds came over as a whole lot less attractive, and we secretly longed for a hedge fund manager or the like to take us under his or her benevolent wing.

Accumulated mythology plays a large part in an ageing club, and the scorebook is there both to inform and correct it. And, although each match is theoretically an island entire of itself, the truth is that what went on before inevitably provides the backdrop for what is to follow. The previous year, we had rolled them over at Elsted for 95, only to be rolled over for 75 ourselves, when it was our turn to bat.

I was sitting on a sailing boat on the Dutch North Sea coast at the time, and followed the events via a series of texts:

11.53: *Graduate:* Do you know where my kit is? xx

12.22: *Roger:* Where you left it (*annoying smiley face*). x

15.47: *Graduate:* Just took 5–14. All clean bowled. All out for 95. Tom. x

15.49: *Tree Hugger:* We just bowled HBBs out for 95. Even we can't fail to chase this. Richard. PS. Where is the scorebook?

15.49: *Roger:* In my kitchen. Sorry. Good luck.

17.55: *Roger:* So what happened then?

18.35: *Roger:* Anyone out there? What happened?

18.42: *Tree Hugger:* I don't know what you're talking about. All out for 70. I resign. Right now. I hate cricket. R. PS. Whatever he says, your son was out for 2, playing across a straight one.

19.05: *Graduate:* Not even talking about it. We were useless. TH told me to defend and I was caught and bowled off a defensive push. Idiot. Both of us. I hate cricket.

22.42: *Tree Hugger:* I mean it. This is the final straw. I want to quit. R. PS. Put me down for the Easton match, please. And the tour.

22.44: *Land Agent:* Text me if you want the gory details. We lost. Badly. Is that gory enough?

23.06: *Young Farmer:* We lost, in case you didn't hear.

23.58:   *Sieve*: Ooops!

In a club of substance and resource, that performance would be the prelude for selecting a stronger batting line this time round, but with the White Hunters, you get whoever volunteers in the lead up, plus who you bully on the day to make up the numbers, and then you make the best of it. It isn't so much a question of which bowler should bowl when, so much as whether the side can actually deliver thirty-five overs at all.

By the Friday before the match, we had eleven on the team sheet, of whom one 'didn't know' if he was going to a wedding that day, but would be sure to let us know, and one 'was pretty certain' he would be back from an airport run with his daughter by the time we started, but would 'keep us informed'. What impresses club captains like me most of all when we go to somewhere like Lords to watch a Test match is not the hallowed turf, not the aching beauty of it all, not even the sense of history seeping through every brick and buttress; it is the knowledge that the skipper out there won't have spent all morning on the telephone trying to persuade his niece's South African boyfriend to turn out, and promising that he doesn't have to pay the match fee and can bat wherever he likes if he does.

If, as a nation, we ever reintroduce conscription, all they would need to do is fill the recruiting offices with retired club captains, and the job would be as good as done.

But eleven is eleven, and I switched off my phone so that the four of us, home together for the first time in months, could go to the pub and not have to worry about who was now remembering that he had failed to tell his other half about his Sunday plans, and was preparing to face the consequences.

At supper, I told them all about the new woman in my life.

'She's called Alison. She's an engineer. She bats and keeps

wicket for Ropley Women, and she said that she thought we might be a bit more fun.'

The post of wicket-keeper had been a problem for the club ever since Nick had left us all those years ago, the unspoken deal being that the Sieve took the gloves if no one else could prize them off him in time. To have a new player who actually advertised themselves as a keeper was luxury indeed, and we allowed ourselves to imagine an amateur Sarah Taylor standing up to the medium pacers, and whipping off the bails as we forced our way through to yet another victory.

'You haven't actually met her yet, let alone watched her play. She might not be as good as you think.' Caroline was more than aware of my capacity to count chickens before the hen had even completed her basic evolution, let alone laid her first egg.

'But it's nice that you've got a woman playing for you at last.'

The 'at last' was heartfelt, and had a very long pedigree, possibly a third of a century. Granted, we had substituted the odd woman in when someone was injured, and even featured one or two in unchallenging roles during evening beer matches over the years, but none had ever signed up for us before, still less paid their membership subs. Sadly, it is not that we were sexist, but that women seemed to find they had better things to do with their time than hang around with us in the middle of a close-mown field for hour after hour.

But it was also a sign of how things were changing in my own mind, if not the wider game. As with bishops and cabinet ministers, so with cricketers: at a time of declining participation, what the hell was the point of depriving your team of fifty per cent of all that potential out there? If she wanted to be part of us, and do what we did, who were we to discourage her?

The unspoken sacrifice within the asymmetry of a family with all boys, or all girls, is made by the parent who does not share their children's gender. Although we had made a deal before we even got married that Caroline shouldn't ever feel she had to come to a game, let alone prepare a match tea, the reality of my doing this sport each summer was her being home alone a good deal.

So, whilst I would sling my kit bag in the car on a Sunday morning, with the anticipation of adventure in my soul, her reality was to turn around and go back to the routine of whatever needed doing at home, or in the garden. And when the boys were old enough, and keen enough, to start coming to the matches themselves as well, her available company was reduced to the dogs.

As with thousands like her, Caroline is happy enough to see her men off the streets and enjoying themselves, but much happier when they come back home again, something that heroic returning cricketers would do well to remember. Especially when they use the salt, pepper and mustard pots at supper to explain graphically how they successfully set a leg trap that afternoon for the Breeder's short ball.

That bit, she just adores.

ON the day of the match, the Tree Hugger and I left everyone in the Hambro Arms at Milton Abbas for their beer and sandwiches, and headed to the new ground early to make sure it was all ready, and that we had a little bit of thinking time. Such was its magnificence, when we first saw it, that all either of us could offer was a couple of tame expletives, plus a stated determination not to be swept away as we had been last year.

The tragedy of the White Hunters is that the sight of a new and beautiful ground, all mown, marked out and ready for the business of the day, so often turns out also to be its high-water mark, as well. It is like laughter coming from another room, or half-heard music filtering across a Mediterranean bay at dusk, in the sense that all of it, or none of it, could be yours if only you could unlock its secrets.

It is an acre of ground that should be glorified by great things happening upon it, not defiled by the failure of an awful dismissal or a soft, dropped catch. Sometimes, it is almost impossible to believe that we can be anything other than magnificent, just as how hittable every ball seems when we spectate.

The Tree Hugger and I walked out to inspect the wicket, an exercise that our lack of real expertise limited to a general view as to how nice it looked out there, which was very, and how agreeable the view was. We decided that, if we won the toss, we would ask them to bat first; there had been heavy overnight rain, which meant that we would theoretically be batting with the benefit of a drying outfield, and, besides, we couldn't imagine that we would be incompetent two years running in our chase. We furtively threw an old ball down onto the middle of the wicket a couple of times, so that anyone who happened to be watching might mistake us for experts searching for signs of variable bounce and carry.

Normally this routine would make my heart beat faster, as I imagined the coming game, but there was no doubt that I was changing. The little pilot light of personal ambition that secretly, however incongruously, wanted me to be the star, had stuttered and gone out. What I really wanted at the moment was simply to be there, with my mates, and do the best I could.

I had spent so many years worrying about where I would slot myself in the batting order – basically low enough to avoid bowlers who were fast, fresh and intimidating, but high enough to have a chance of affecting the outcome – and now, suddenly, I didn't seem to care so much. Just at the point that I was committing myself to becoming better both in mind and body, the need for it was drifting out to sea.

We looked north towards the gate, and saw a convoy of cars driving towards us, and disgorging passengers with the cheerful air of people who didn't necessarily subscribe to modern-day *no alcohol before sports* theories. The skipper came out to join us in the middle and obligingly called wrong when I tossed the coin.

'You can have first dig,' I told him. I had heard David Lloyd call it this from time to time on Sky TV, and it sounded rather workmanlike and professional, in a gritty Lancastrian way.

'I'm sorry?' said David, genuinely confused.

'Dig,' I said. 'You can have the first one.'

'I'm terribly sorry. I really don't know what you are talking about.'

'Er. Bat. You can bat.' It wasn't working. I was who I was.

'Ahhh. You should have said.'

We had abandoned our habitual 'not out first ball' rule for the day, as it nearly always seemed to work against us, rather than for us, and, anyway, we were beginning to think we were better than that. This was to be the real stuff. And, once again, we bowled at them beautifully, restricting them to a total of 150 runs for us to chase at a rate substantially under five runs an over. At various stages we even had outswing from one end and inswing from the other, and then raw pace available from the Young Farmer and the Graduate when that had run its course.

The Ginger even put down four tidy overs and during the course of them gained two lbw decisions despite appealing for neither himself, presumably on the basis that excessive noise was an unwelcome distraction to the thoughtful mind. Alison, the

Engineer, in keeping wicket for us for the first time, looked the part, and occasionally she even *was* the part, but with just enough byes and misfields for us to believe that she had found her level.

I gently marshalled things from my private position at first slip, reddening in the June sun, and idly wondering what could possibly go wrong.

Once again, I didn't have to wonder for long. The answer was 'quite a lot', and 'quite quickly'.

The Graduate, who had scored a brutal forty last time he played, and the Tree Hugger, who had looked peerless in the nets, opened for us – with the same result as at Arundel, but with eight more runs and six more balls between them. Our number three lasted two balls, and our number four one less than that. Much was expected of the Engineer on her first outing, but much remained to be delivered as she made her way back to the pavilion a few balls later, caught in the slips off an injudicious drive.

In contrast to Arundel, it was generally good bowling rather than awful shot selection that was our downfall, and the procession of wickets continued, my own included, until we were 26 for eight and, once again in sight of our lowest ever score. Not for the first time, we had been duped by the sight of a sub-continental cricketer coming on to bowl into thinking that his deliveries would be sly, slow and spinning, rather than fast and moving both in the air, and off the seam. Which is what they did. And they had wrecked the heart of our innings.

To say that the arrival of the Sieve at the wicket in these circumstances, and as the last but one batsman, was a reassuring prospect, would be simply untrue. More Mister Bean than Marshall Blucher, we knew from long experience that he had all the defensive technique of a silky anteater.

However, from now on, it was all about him and the Young

Farmer, possibly the most unlikely heroic partnership since avocado and burned bacon. The Young Farmer, who was part of the backbone of our batting, and had been since he was sixteen, and the Sieve who, well, wasn't. They had 130 balls to try to survive and allow the draw, with only the last man to come; and the last man was the Ginger, who hadn't picked up a bat in anger, or any other emotion for that matter, for nine months. I opted for a ringside seat at this festival of the bizarre, and volunteered to go and umpire the remainder of the match.

I quietly reminded the Sieve of his net session down in Southampton all those weeks ago, and how well it had gone, and the Young Farmer spoke briefly to him about only trying to make contact with balls that would otherwise hit his bat or pad, and never looking for quick singles. The Sieve took it all in with the delighted look on his face of the keen boy scout who has accidentally pitched up in an action zone, and was finally about to be called upon to dig something out of a horse's hoof. People can change, we assured him, and this was time for his own metamorphosis, possibly into a less permeable kitchen gadget.

We wondered how long it would take the opposition to remember that he possessed but two shots, plus an underused 'leave'. Early balls were more about luck than survival, as he tracked down and hauled in his concentration and radar; the first one he actually hit went in the air, but plopped harmlessly into no-man's-land. Feet planted to the crease like the statue of Ozymandias in the desert sand, he started to lunge forward to the ball, no matter what length it had been bowled, and then gradually started to make contact.

After twenty of the 120 balls, the Young Farmer was on about eight, and the Sieve was yet to score, but everyone knew this was about the latter, not the former in his reliable excellence, and it was about the late-flowering triumph of mediocrity. From time to time some base instinct would bring out the wafting bat, and we would all shut our eyes and hold our breath till the danger was gone.

Time passed. Balls were ticked off. Runs were spurned. As the sun dipped down towards the wooded hill to our west, the match entered a phase that was beyond metaphor. Whatever the opposite of putting an attack to the sword might be, the Sieve was doing it magnificently, and to huge effect. Fielders, who had at first been delighted to see the arrival of the genial number ten bat at the crease, found their joy moving via amused tolerance to scarcely disguised impatience as block by block, he saw off or missed every offering that was delivered his way.

With eight overs left, they declared the joke over and brought back the opening bowlers to force a quick end to proceedings, which had the initial effect of bringing both batsmen to the middle of the wicket to punch gloves and re-discuss tactics. But where they might have expected a breakthrough, they got a more determined version of the same. Playing and missing as often as he hit the ball, the Sieve just stood there and let it all happen.

By the time they had three overs left, the Young Farmer had scored around thirty, but the Sieve was still, triumphantly, in the low single figures. The fielders tightened the noose around him, but he continued to see them off. If everyone eventually rises to the level of their own incompetence, as the Peter Principle asserts, the Sieve had soared through his own, and shot out the lights above him into the bargain.

Three balls before the end, they got him. A man can only avoid his fate for so long, and over so many times, and he had done so for more than an hour and for about seventy balls. He simply played across a straight one and was bowled. He had probably spent longer out in the middle in that one visit to the crease than the aggregate of his last ten seasons, and he was almost beyond consolation not to have seen it through.

It cannot be usual for a man to receive a standing ovation when he has scored the grand total of three runs, but he did, not because he had, but because of the manner in which he had scored them. In an echo of my own journey, he had found the other 'him' exactly when he needed it most. It was neither pretty, nor excellent, but it was beyond priceless. The look of misery on his face as he came in said it all; he simply felt that he had let the side down in not seeing it through.

Two balls to go, and all the Ginger had to do was keep them out. No one had told him that we were not playing the 'not out first ball' rule, or he had been asleep when they had, and he smacked the first back over the bowler's head for a one-bounce four in celebration of what he thought was a free hit.

This brought the Young Farmer down the wicket to explain that, if he valued his wellbeing, all he had to do was to try his hardest not to get out to the one remaining ball. In the event, it passed harmlessly under his bat, and we had squeaked a draw from nowhere. It's not the kind of satisfactory ending that you could have explained away to a Martian, but it was as sweet to us as any thumping victory we had ever had.

In the bar that evening, the events of the day were lived and relived, and then burnished, polished and recycled, until it was clear to all that they would take their place in the highest level of the club's thirty-three-year collective memory. Like the wild boar incident on the first French tour, and the gloveless wicket-keeper in a riverside Somerset village, the Sieve's innings had been elevated to the halls of the club's mythology, where they most surely belonged. And mythology is a lot of why we do it.

As the evening progressed, we put the finishing touches to the plans for the finale of our season, our French Tour. This was to be a fourth return for us to the Lot Valley in the Dordogne, but was to take place for the first time this year in October. Who was coming along, who we were playing, where we were staying and where we were eating all came under collective discussion, as did the thorny old question of whether we took along twelve players, on the basis that one of the 'pensioners' would probably get crocked, and we would have a spare; or eleven, and know that everyone would play in both games, whatever. Either way, it was joy stretching out into the middle distance.

The Graduate, many beers later, was mentally in the Dordogne already, sorting out the batting order and explaining his concept of the 'ring of steel' field that he would deploy on some bit of matting in Southern France in a dozen weeks' time. But that's the thing with the Graduate. I thought back to a wet holiday morning fifteen or so years before, when he had raced through the entire Plymouth Aquarium in about six minutes, past every exhibit, every notice board, every video screen, because someone had told him there was a shark at the end, and a gift shop after that.

Seeing the shark had become for him an imperative that subdued everything else into irrelevance, so that his entire memory of the experience is now presumably a blur with a large set of teeth at the end of it. Afterwards we had sat him down with an ice cream in the car park and talked to him about enjoying what he had, right here, right now, and not always running on for the next thing.

Living in the moment had proved to be an easier concept to explain to others than to practise myself over the years, and I didn't even have the promise of a shark. But much of this year was about exactly that: understanding that we are blessed indeed to have the shared endeavour of team sports into our seventh decade, doubly so if it is with our own children. With this in mind, there is no point in doing anything other than smiling for as long as the face muscles hold out.

Meanwhile, from within the comforting normality of its defeats, mishaps and occasional triumphs, this season was beginning to look much like its thirty-two predecessors, and I found myself wishing that I minded more.

7 The Flowers of Middle Summer

August

AND then in August, they all go away.

The enthusiasm and momentum of the early season gives way to the family holiday in North Cornwall, inter-railing in south-eastern Europe, or camping in the midge fields of the Hebrides, and suddenly it becomes five times more difficult to gather a team together. I once found myself calling the eleventh player on our team five minutes after we had been due to start a particular match, only to hear the cry of seagulls in the background, and the unmistakable sound of rich French children screaming their way down Mediterranean water sides.

'Are you nearly here?' I asked with ironic bitterness from my cloudy Hampshire valley, only for the phone to go dead on me for about a month.

And the extraordinary thing about it all is that all the bowlers seem to go away for the same fortnight, followed by all the batsmen a few weeks later, which leads in turn to a month of teams that can either make 250, but can't take a wicket, or can bowl a team out for thirty-five, but can't get halfway there when it is their turn to respond. A few of our older members, friendless and misguided, have taken up cycling, and they in turn choose August to enter criteria, time trials, eroicas and grand tours on busy cricket weekends. These are dark times.

But still the matches come, and still we never learn.

THE Tree Hugger was captaining the next match, a Sunday fixture against a local team that had consistently circled the plughole of not quite measuring up as an agreeable opposition, and therefore getting dropped, but had somehow always avoided it. They had the word 'gentlemen' in their name and, in our long experience, anyone who had that, wasn't.

Our home fixtures are quite few and far between these days, so it is always a bit of a sadness when the wrong team manages to snaffle one of them. Here is an idiot's guide of how to spot them:

- THEY don't come to the pub before the match, or after it. Instead, they climb into their executive cars and head home to wives whom we like to think hate them.

- THE beauty of our home ground passes them by, as does the fact of our hosts having worked their socks off for the last few days to prepare it for them. 'Where are the showers?' is all they can think of to say when they arrive.

- WHILST our idea of a good day is the utilitarian concept of 'maximum benefit for maximum number of people', theirs is the rational egoism of someone called Dave batting out the full thirty-five overs without retiring, thus denying anyone else an innings, and then marking the achievement of his century by glaring humourlessly at his bat, and taking a fresh guard.

- THEIR umpires defy the laws of cricket, and their scorers often defy the laws of basic mathematics.

- THEY look at you in stunned incomprehension when you ask for a small match fee to cover the day. 'I'll have to see what I can do,' they reply, as if it's all your fault. Indeed, as if the Fall of Man is all your fault.

So we play at least one of them every year, not because we enjoy it, but because it allows the iron to enter our souls a little bit, and helps us appreciate how nice everyone else is.

As is the way with men of a certain age, my children had contrived to be making their way towards the match from geographically extreme places, and after socially extreme activities, relying on an unlikely chain of kindness, bribery, favours and public transport to get them to within spitting distance of the ground.

Even in an age of plenty, let alone an age of austerity, getting to our ground without a car is something of a challenge. When an unfortunate member of a visiting team collapsed whilst retrieving the ball from the fine leg boundary during an evening match some years ago, it took forty-five minutes for the first of three ambulances to converge from the nearest town, by which time the player was not only dead, but initial plans had already been made for both his funeral, and for the subsequent unveiling of the memorial bench at his home ground during the return match the following summer. As a club, we might not always be in the vanguard of cricketing excellence, but we like to think we know a thing or two about using available time wisely.

A text arrived from the Ginger just before I left home. 'Feel a bit like shit. Is it still on?' It was followed by one from the Wealth Manager. 'Slightly overdid last night. Got a reserve?' Having answered with a curt and authoritative 'yes' and 'no' respectively, I fell to thinking once again that these were not the kind of issues that Joe Root found himself dealing with in the lead up to a match. I mean, would James Anderson go out and get bladdered the night before an Ashes test?

Rather than drive over on my own, I offered a lift to the Beekeeper, partly because he is genial company, but mainly because he has a beard of great excellence. Being unable to grow a proper beard myself, I have always admired people who can, and I tend to cosy up to them on the off-chance some of the masculinity will rub off on me. Because he runs a fruit and veg business in Covent Garden, where all the work is done at night, every cricket match we have ever played is during his version of night-time, which explains why he is so violently inconsistent, but possibly not why he ended up supporting Norwich.

Besides, he and I keep two beehives together, and we can fill any hour with which we are provided with meaningless talk about 're-queening' and preventative treatment for the Varroa virus. Every big decision we have taken on behalf of our 100 thousand little tenants has been taken on, or near to, a cricket pitch. Whilst, ironically, every cricketing conversation we have takes place from the depths of beekeeping suits and veils, up to our eyes in frames and irritated bees.

He was in trouble at home, having failed to tell his wife about the match until about ten minutes before I picked him up, and he asked me to stop at a florist so that he could buy an over-priced tied bunch of lilies by way of a peace offering.

'Isn't that a bit obvious?' I asked, as he climbed back in the car.

'It needs to be bloody obvious,' he said. 'Afrikaners don't do subtle, so this has got absolutely nothing to do with love, and everything to do with being fed this evening.' He was nothing if not practical.

At the ground, the Tree Hugger had already got into a misunderstanding with the opposition captain over the 'not out first ball' rule we liked to apply, and over individuals retiring when they had reached fifty. Viewed from the boundary while they were out in the middle for the toss, their body language was redolent of two maiden aunts who loathed each other, but had been thrown together in icy politeness for Christmas lunch.

'We're batting,' he said, as he came back to the pavilion, and told the Ginger and me to pad up.

'I'm happy to bat at eleven,' said the former hopelessly. The hangover and the general excesses of the last twenty-four hours were meeting round the back of his skull, and were creating havoc.

'No. I want you to open,' said the Tree Hugger irritably. He didn't have children himself, and so didn't realise that, whilst it was a brave move, it might also have consequences. Besides, the

Ginger was his godson, which complicated things.

'Do you want a guard?' asked the Graduate, who was umpiring, before the first ball was bowled.

'No, thanks,' said the Ginger miserably, and the opening bowler strode to the end of his mark with the air of a hyena that has picked up the scent of a wounded zebra.

'Have him!' said the skipper unpleasantly. 'On the stumps, Smithy.'

The first ball was a short one and, although the Ginger had the protection of a helmet, I worried momentarily for his safety. After all, he could hardly stand, still less face quick bowling. But his reluctant bat somehow swung round in a lazy arc, connected, and the ball soared over the square boundary and into the hayfield beyond for six.

Smithy walked back to his mark alongside the skipper, clearly plotting something. The something, when it came, was a viciously short one just outside the off stump, which took the shoulder of the Ginger's bat and flew over the slips for four. Smithy glared at the Ginger, who smiled genially back.

'Good wheels, Smithy,' said the keeper. ''Ave 'im next time.'

The third ball was duly delivered in the form of a toe-breaking yorker on middle and leg, at which the Ginger weakly prodded, and deflected just enough to send off down to fine leg for another boundary. Fourteen off three balls.

'Nice areas, Smithy,' said the keeper with slightly less conviction. 'Too good for the ginger.'

The Ginger turned and smiled at him, agreeing that it had, indeed, been too good for him.

Once again, the skipper escorted Smithy back to his mark with his arm round his shoulder. The Graduate, never at a loss for chipping in with a helpful comment, alerted them that his brother hadn't actually woken up yet, and they could only expect the run rate to increase from here on once he had. It was a prediction borne out by the next ball, another short one, at which the Ginger swished nauseously, only to top-edge it over the keeper for another six.

Twenty off the first four balls of the match, all from the bat of a man who hadn't practised in years, didn't want to play anyway, and was eyeing up the boundary only as a reconnaissance for when he needed to run off and throw up. For those of us who had practised night after night in the close season, it was a salutary moment.

'Nice levers, Al,' offered the umpiring Graduate, in an echo of the fielding side's jargon, before calling the next ball a wide, as the bowler in his fury had fired it down two foot outside the leg stump and way out of the reach of the wicket-keeper, on its way to the fence by the logpile. Twenty-five off four legal balls, and the first over wasn't yet finished. In thirty years of our club, we had never had a start so muscular in its effect, and yet so unintentional from the point of view of the batsman. It was an enormous relief to the latter that the next ball clattered into his off stump, ending both his own torment, and that of the bowler.

'Well batted, mate,' said the one genial person in the fielding side to the retreating ginger, a compliment that died a slow death in the sterility of a team that simply didn't get the joke.

Out came the Beekeeper, and studiously blocked out the final ball of the first over, which a glance at the scoreboard confirmed had gone for twenty-five haphazard, but glorious, runs.

After an over or two, he wandered down the wicket to talk to me; I assumed about bees, as that was all we ever really talked about. A mid-wicket conference was often the perfect place to iron out some of the finer points of the following week's hive inspection.

'You look like a goldfish,' he said.

'What do you mean?' This wasn't polite, and it certainly wasn't anything to do with bees, let alone cricket.

'You look terrified. You've been out here for three overs and you haven't scored a run. You're just prodding at it, as if it's going to explode.' He lifted his bat to his shoulder, and fired an imaginary shot at a passing pigeon. 'Just go back to thwacking it, won't you? The old you scored more runs. And was more fun. Just saying.'

He had a point. In the good old days, I could be relied on to score quickly, or get out, or both. These days, the coaching had made me so transfixed about doing the technically correct thing, that I had become a walking run desert, clinging on to my innings like a sloth to the underside of a Cecropia tree, and frustrating my teammates into the bargain. I had only two ears, and my current problem was that one was being used up hearing the things my cricket coach might be saying to me, and the other one tuned in to my sports psychologist. There were no ears left to hear the rustling of reality in the trees and, to make matters worse, my yoga classes were making me try to project a zen-like calm that I certainly didn't feel.

Halfway back to his crease, he wandered back down towards me.

'Also, you're sticking your bum out while you're waiting for the ball to be delivered. It just looks so wrong.' He wandered back to his crease and absent-mindedly carted the opening bowler over mid-wicket for another six.

'Come in on the one for me, Jack,' shouted the skipper. Young Jack did as he was told, and watched the next delivery sail over his head to the precise point where he had been so recently standing. All of which meant that we were racing along in the sunshine, and that our fifty came up in only the fifth over, of which my contribution was precisely zero.

'I'll bring you a crate of strawberries if you hit your next ball for six,' called the Beekeeper loudly from the other end of the pitch. Being a Covent Garden man, every bet he made was based on the promise of seasonal fruit and its derivatives. Smithy overheard the exchange and completely lost his cool, firing in the next ball wildly, and sending it soaring over both my head, and the chubby wicket-keeper's as well.

'A punnet!' he shouted down the wicket 'I'll buy you a punnet. It only went for four, and the crate was for if you hit it.'

By the time the Beekeeper was out at 78 for two, my personal tally was still just four. The Engineer, the Sieve and the Tree Hugger all came and went, and still all I could think of doing was eliminating any risk of getting out. My score gradually rose through a series of edges and misfields until, when I had made twenty and the overall score was 180 for five, I skied the first aggressive hit I had made to a height that anyone on the pitch could have caught it, including the lady trotting by on a horse.

'Boring wanker,' I heard the keeper say, as I headed off to the pavilion.

'Yep. There's one in every team, Jim. But he was special.' I found myself wanting to agree with them both.

And on it all went in the glorious sunshine, culminating in the Graduate repeating what he had seen Jos Buttler doing at the Oval the weekend before, and lapping a bowler, albeit a terribly slow one, over the wicket-keeper's head and into the sycamore woods beyond fine leg.

'What did you think of that?' he asked the umpire.

It was the last ball of our innings, and we had made 285 for seven, the second-highest score in our history. And we didn't even have a strong batting side.

ALTHOUGH we don't get a huge amount of opportunity for complacency in the White Hunters, we normally grasp it to our chests with love and affection when it presents itself. This makes a big score, ironically, rather trickier to defend than a small one. The Tree Hugger and I, whichever of us happens to be skippering for the day, are apt to indulge in flights of fancy if things look too good, try out inadvisable schemes and, worst of all, bowl an over or two ourselves. The theory is fine: assume control of a game, take your foot off the gas for a bit to 'make a better game of it', and then re-establish control when things start to turn.

The only problem is that this is the precise time that the strike bowler pulls a hamstring, and his colleague suddenly forgets how to control his component body parts. And the unchallengeable position starts to go to good, then merely promising, before descending through problematic and finally coming to rest in the lush grasslands of abject defeat. And we have learned the hard way that snatching defeat from the jaws of victory is a turd that really cannot be polished.

So, it was without surprise that I noticed the Young Farmer and the Graduate surrounding the Tree Hugger during the tea break, and extracting from him a pledge that he wouldn't chuck it away.

I also overheard the visiting skipper telling his opening bat, while he was padding up, that 'the bird is keeping', which, he assured them 'should be good for a laugh'. It was too tempting an intervention not to be shared among us, and for him to be aware that we knew about.

For the first few overs, it looked like they would overhaul our score in next to no time, as the chubby wicket-keeper and his opening partner got amongst our bowling with a vengeance. The Graduate, no wallflower when it came to on-pitch liveliness, was ratcheting up his journey through the gazette of unsubtle asides, with the obvious effect that the crosser he became, the more chaotic his bowling got.

It was only after a handful of overs, as another ball streaked through an untenanted part of the field on its way to the point boundary, that he exclaimed to no one in particular that it was like bowling to a team of only five fielders. It got me thinking, and the thinking got me counting. He was right in his general suspicion, and a simple head count by me and verified by the Sieve, fresh from his own career-defining two (not out), confirmed that someone was missing. A more detailed head count by the Tree Hugger revealed that the missing player was the Ginger, whom no one could remember seeing since the beginning of tea.

Brother, father and godfather all made their hurried point that they could not be held responsible for an adult human being, whatever the others said, and we continued the game for a while with the slightly uneasy backdrop of there being an officially 'missing person'. A few balls later, the obese wicket-keeper flailed the Young Farmer high and far into the adjacent woods, to be followed by the Wealth Manager, climbing over the fence like a plump royal bride climbing ever so delicately into her carriage.

After a minute or two, a voice came out of the foliage.

'I've found him!' it said. 'He's fast asleep.'

And he was right. There, in the privacy of a bed of camomile and herb robert, the Ginger had laid his head and was sleeping the sleep of the devastatingly tanked-up. If you listened and watched very carefully, he was snoring and smacking his lips gently together like a tired bear that has nonetheless come across a small trace of honey. It seemed almost cruel to spoil it for him.

'Get your arse back out here!' shouted the Graduate from the boundary's edge, in the direct way that brother traditionally feels free to communicate with brother. And very slowly, very deliberately, the Ginger arrived back on the pitch, blinking into the sunshine, holding his hand up by way of an apology, more as if he had been unavoidably detained for a couple of seconds than he had been fast asleep in the woods for the last hour.

As the late afternoon wore on, and unshackled by captaincy, I found myself observing proceedings as if from a distance, and starting to drift away from some of the changes I had mentally signed up to at the beginning of the year. The match was slowly, but decisively, swinging in our direction, as each unsmiling batsman replaced the last one out in the middle. Player for player, and in the basic imperative of wanting the victory, they amounted to far more cricketing prowess than we did. But, for all our occasional incompetence, we clearly liked being with each other, and were therefore able to amount to more than the sum of our parts.

We had achieved that hardest of tricks of integrating the next generation into the club without altering whatever its essential DNA happened to be: they enabled us to be better, but they didn't change us. It therefore started to strike me as borderline weird that I had spent so much of the last six months trying to change myself and, by extension, the team.

It was somehow inevitable that the Ginger would have a hand in the closing rites of the match. For most of the afternoon, he had been a shadowy physical presence on the pitch, if not an intellectual one. The Tree Hugger had hidden him in fielding positions of little or no consequence, so that he could complete the recovery that had started with his little sleep in the herb robert. By the time eight wickets were down, he had been moved up to slip, not because we needed a slip for the Tree Hugger's gentle offerings, but because he could complete his reintegration into society by chatting to the Engineer behind the stumps.

With over a hundred runs to spare and only two wickets to

take, the Tree Hugger had introduced himself into the attack, and had been taken for two boundaries with some enthusiasm in his first couple of balls by the facing batsman. The third ball, which would have been called a wide had the batsman not decided to move a yard out to the offside to biff it to the point boundary, contrived to deceive him into offering an edge, which the Engineer pouched, albeit on the third attempt.

The dismissal brought the skipper to the wicket, behind a bow wave of delicious ironic potential, including the fact that he clearly didn't rate the 'bird' behind the stumps, and that he had specifically refused to play the 'not out first ball' rule. This, we felt, was very much not the situation he had in mind when he had shouted at his dog, and left his relieved wife at the kitchen sink a few short hours before.

The next ball from the Tree Hugger was a repeat of the previous one, only worse. It was slow and loopy and, once again, the umpire was readying his arms to signal it as a wide, and, once again, the batsman should have left it, but didn't. This time, he got a thick outside edge, which rose sharply towards the Engineer's face.

Partly out of self-preservation, and possibly partly through some residual sense of outrage at the boorish sexism with which he had referenced her, she raised her right glove towards her head and tried to grab it. But it was spinning fairly violently away from her all the time, and she only succeeded in parrying it towards the lone slip, but not close enough for it to be a likely catch.

Sometimes, however, things happen because karma dictates it. Having been virtually incapable of voluntary movement for the previous five hours of cricket, the Ginger suddenly launched himself leftwards and downwards towards the rapidly falling ball and, by the thinnest of thin margins, managed to get his fingers underneath it, and not drop it. There was a stunned silence.

'It didn't carry,' said the skipper immediately, and re-marked his crease with his bat, as if to denote that he was going nowhere. The Ginger said nothing, but stared at him enigmatically.

'You what?' said the Young Farmer, striding in towards the action.

I waited for the protests that would inevitably arise from the normally passive Hunters once they had grasped what was going on, but another voice intervened.

'It did, mate. You're out.' It was the presiding umpire who, hours ago, had been the lone fielding voice to have congratulated 'the Ginger' for his innings.

'I'm afraid he's right,' added the square leg umpire. 'I watched it all the way in.'

Wordlessly, the skipper tucked his bat under his arm and marched off, and probably only I noticed the raised eyes and shrugs that passed between the two umpires.

And the man who had put the least possible visible effort into the game was the man who put the final nail in the coffin, reminding everyone in the process how much of a role random chance still plays, and why that is a wonderful thing.

'WHAT you said to me about me being more fun in the old days,' I said to the Beekeeper as casually as I could, as we drove home after celebrating our comprehensive victory. 'Did you mean that?'

'Course I did,' he said. 'Your problem is that, for some reason, you're over-thinking it all this season, and trying to be a cricketer.' He lit an enormous cigar that he had bought in the pub after his third pint, and filled the car with what he took to be the delight of its smoke. I wanted to protest, but somehow it didn't seem the right moment.

'That's not what we love you for.'

'And that would be?'

'You're crap. But you and Tree Hugger organise it all. That's what we love you for. So, go back to how you were, please.'

I pulled into his driveway, and waited for him to get out, giving him the opportunity to say that he had been joking.

'Seriously,' he said with a warm smile, and carried his limp bunch of flowers to the irritated Afrikaner waiting within.

8 Village Politics

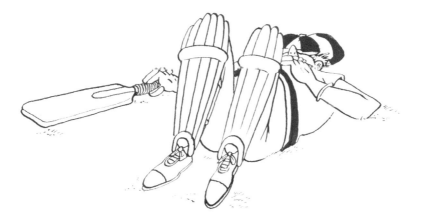

August

It was honey time.

After three years of being bad, then indifferent, and finally just-about-average apiarists, the Beekeeper and I had hit the jackpot. Bees are sensitive little things, and the endless fine weather of the previous two months had encouraged them to concentrate on turning nectar and pollen into honey, rather than sulking, swarming or razzing up the neighbourhood, as they tended to do in wet summers. We had been joined on the terrace in our little production line of de-capping, spinning, decanting, filtering and jarring by my wife, Caroline, and the Tree Hugger, and the talk had turned by degrees from our bees, to local gossip and finally to cricket.

'Why don't you let someone else skipper the West Heath match next week,' suggested the Beekeeper, after the Tree Hugger and I had done our normal rant about recruitment and drop-outs. 'Give someone else responsibility.'

Most years, we tried this at least once, and the effect was normally, if anything, more catastrophic than when it was either of us. The Breeder did it a couple of times, but tended to forget halfway through the game that it was him making decisions, and he would start waiting for people to suggest things, or to give him orders themselves. Conversely, the Wealth Manager and Land Agent treated the burden of high office like teenagers driving a sports car, taking outrageous risks in an effort to push the whole thing to the wire in the last over, normally to dismal failure.

Some would be toe-curlingly nice, and do all that they could to avoid offending anyone, even if it meant certain defeat; whilst others took it as a God-given chance to put right the inadequacy of their school years, and shouted at people to make the point that they could. Rational family men would often morph into drooling dictators when the opportunity of unchallenged leadership was presented to them.

Most of our players, however, refused point blank, and would go and hide in the changing room until the risk of infection had passed, and it was safe to re-emerge as an anonymous number. Contrary to popular belief, anonymous numbers are what most social cricketers are happiest to be.

'What about you?' Caroline asked the Beekeeper. We could have saved her the effort, as he had always insisted that his mind was stuffed too full of brassicas, soft fruit and late nights to allow the intrusion of something like leadership. And then there was always that beard.

'No,' he said definitively, as he drained the last of the contents of the spinner. 'Let the Graduate have a go.'

At first sight, it was not an avenue that either of us had planned to go down, but the more time we gave it, the less ridiculous it looked. In a way, giving the captaincy to someone who was, himself, one of the trickier captaincy challenges, was the ultimate act of poacher turned gamekeeper.

'Oh, that's nice!' said his mother, in the mistaken impression that her firstborn had climbed a rung on one of life's great career ladders. 'I'll wash his jersey.'

THE Graduate, who had been interested in leadership since acquiring a younger brother to boss around twenty years before, took about four nano-seconds of persuasion before he accepted the poisoned chalice, and, as his father, I knew well enough that whoever else's advice he needed on the subject, it was not mine. It was one of those curious bits of family dynamics that dictated, whether he wanted it or not, he would be given advice, and, whether I gave it or not, he would assume he knew what it would be.

So I wrote and printed off a list of long-harvested thoughts, and stuck them in the sports section of the Saturday newspaper that I knew he would read when he was home later in the weekend. Even though he would guess immediately who had put it there, its presumed anonymity would make it like one of Donald Rumsfeld's 'known unknowns' and therefore acceptable.

The desiderata of social cricket captaincy:

- GO placidly amid the noise and haste. *You are not in charge; you are merely responsible. There is a big difference.*

- EXERCISE caution in your business affairs, for the world is full of trickery. *The unseen but enthusiastically foreshadowed ringer that you are relying on for six probing overs and forty runs will be utterly useless. Always.*

- LISTEN to others, even the dull and ignorant; they too have their story. *The fat bloke who volunteered at the party last night, and who is merely making up the numbers without any real involvement, once took five South African wickets for Namibia. If you don't try, you will never know.*

- ENJOY your achievements as well as your plans. *However, unlike the rest of life, where you only regret what you didn't try, in cricket, you will normally regret just about everything you did try.*

- TAKE kindly the council of the years. *The minute you move second slip out, a soft, slow and insultingly easy catch will present itself to where he has just been standing. Normally next ball.*

- NURTURE strength of spirit to shield you from sudden misfortune. *No. No one else on either side thought to put the urn on for tea forty minutes ago. That was your job, whatever else happened to be on your to-do list, and they will all stare at you when they drink cold tea. And they would like you to magically produce drinks halfway through the innings, too, even if you are the fielding captain.*

- REMEMBER what peace there may be in silence. *That person who you stuck at number eleven because he said, 'Don't worry, Skip. Put me where you like. I don't mind where I go,' does mind. And he will hold a grudge, as will his wife. She will still bring it up three years hence, when you meet in a garden centre.*

- BEYOND a wholesome discipline, be gentle on yourself. *But remember, you haven't actually won until the metaphorical fat lady has sung, left the building, and done her entire weekly shop at Aldi.*

- YOU are a child of the universe. No less than the trees and the stars, you have a right to be here. *However, don't kid yourself. Your job is simply to provide twenty-two people with a lovely afternoon's cricket, and your reward is to be allowed to be one of them. Unless you have miscounted, and recruited one too many, in which case you will be expected to stand down and umpire both innings.*

- BE cheerful. Strive to be happy. *And, at the end of the day, remember that you are simply the nipple of the grease gun that allows the cogs of the season to rotate, and your ideas of Napoleonic grandeur are illusory. You are the servant of the team, and not its master.*

I found out later that the Graduate had also messaged both the Sieve and the Beekeeper for their own advice, neither having ever been left in charge of the asylum themselves, I should point out.

'Inspire the troops, that's all,' advised the Sieve, who was obviously drunk, and reading some of his old Bulldog Drummond stories at the time. The Sieve had a form of mindless optimism that is the sole preserve of the perseveringly inept.

'Dunno,' said the Beekeeper. 'Shouting at people normally seems to do the trick'.

To be fair to the Graduate, he took his responsibilities for the coming match extremely seriously, and copies of batting orders, bowlers to be used and even fielding positions for the coming encounter were left dotted all around the kitchen the weekend before the match. He filled the two vacant spaces with highly competent friends of the absent Ginger, who were on their gap years, and therefore spending the late summer doing enough odd jobs to raise money for that last hurrah in Ibiza before university started, and they had the chance to become genuinely poor and indebted.

As someone who had learned most of his cricketing knowledge from the IPL, and from various instructional websites, the Graduate was one of the sport's great theorists, sometimes hilariously so. He would suggest, for example, during a long, barren spell, that the Breeder deploy the knuckle ball to take pace off and deceive the batsman, only to find that it was a concept so many light years away from anything the Breeder knew about that he would smile vaguely and wander back to his mark with a confused look on his face. All the Breeder knew about knuckles was that pigs had them, and that they were around £5.00 a kilo on the thirty-month futures market.

Into this process, and back from a long trip among the warlords of South Sudan that had precluded his involvement in the early part of the season, shimmered the Gun Runner.

To this day, in the 377 matches that the club has played, the best excuse for non-attendance at a match that we have ever received was a text from the Gun Runner half an hour before play was due to start, that simply said: *Sorry. Gold mine overrun by Sudan People's Liberation Army. Must fly.* Somehow this made the normal fare of ill parents, christenings and school open days seem unforgivably mundane.

His office in London was only half a mile from the Graduate's, and a couple of days before the match, he invited the latter to his club to discuss the finer points of leadership and captaincy, and to brief him how the land lay 'in enemy territory'. No one else in the White Hunters had a London club to which they could invite people, and the Graduate was suitably impressed.

Four hours later, and fifteen units of alcohol and a big West End dinner to the good, he shuffled onto the Tube and back to his digs in Lewisham to mull over the advice he had been given. And, whilst it was not entirely clear to the rest of us that the provision of dodgy hardware to the unsettled natives of the world's flashpoints had much to offer our cricket club, it was very obvious that the Graduate disagreed.

He might not have cherished his father's advice, but he would take it from the Gun Runner in any currency he could get it, and the following morning an email went out to the team:

Morning All. Looking forward to seeing you tomorrow at 1800 GMT (Zulu) at HQ.
Enemy strength assessed as strong but fractious. Local sources indicate their keeper is sleeping with the skipper's wife. Detailed instructions will be issued at the Start Line. Etc.

The anonymity of the 'etc' at the end of the email, which seemed to replace any formal sign off, was beguiling, and appeared to suggest that there was even juicier information to come our way before D-Day. We were all riveted.

Besides, if you took into account the advice the Graduate was already getting from the Sieve, the Beekeeper and me, he would be nothing if not well briefed by the time he took his team to the field the following evening. When an email from the Tree Hugger to the Graduate arrived on my desk, in the form of a blind copy to the effect that he was always available for captaincy advice if it was needed, over fifty per cent of the team were already contributing to the leadership process. It is to the Graduate's credit that he ignored everyone apart from the Gun Runner, whose esoteric contributions he found much to his taste.

Meanwhile I was conducting my own private audit of progress against the various yardsticks I had set myself all those months ago. After today, there would be only five matches left, of which two would be down in the Dordogne, and there wasn't a whole lot of time to tick off the achievements. The hip was certainly better, and with no medical intervention: it was as if the long, hot summer and a reducing regime of violent exercise had done the trick. Months ago, yoga threatened to upset the apple cart, but after a few short weeks it, and I, had come to a mutual understanding that we loathed each other, and would play no further part in each other's lives.

As a team, we hadn't won fifty per cent of our matches so far, as I had hoped we would, but we were at around thirty-five per cent, and that was a great deal better than the season before. Far from rising up to an average at or near thirty, my own batting had gone diametrically in the other direction, and I was enjoying comfortably the worst season of my thirty-two-year career in the club. True, I was tending to be unlucky in the bowlers that I faced when I went out to the middle, but I had created such a tortured backdrop for myself, one in which two different coaches and a sports psychologist were all whispering in my ear simultaneously throughout my conflicted stays at the crease, that I had become a bundle of nerves, and was doomed to fail.

Something deep down *had* changed, though, even if I was still unaware as to what it was.

BY the evening of the match against West Heath, the heatwave had been going on for the best part of two months, with the result that the countryside was parched a curious straw colour, and the wicket had more bounce in it than a student bank card. The outfield, where as recently as the previous summer, we had photographed an extended family of mallard taking up temporary residence in the four inches of water it offered, had the tint and texture of the Serengeti; all that was missing was the annoying circle of safari vehicles full of German tourists filming the leopard family group nearby.

It occurred to us more than once during the season that, whilst we all spent decades dreaming of summers like this, where the cricket would never be rained off – when we actually had one, we didn't know what to do with it. We would stand out in the middle, plastered in factor 50 that would sweat down into our eyes, complaining about chafing and trying to remember how to deal with a sharply rising ball.

The best bit was that you could sit in the pub garden in your shirtsleeves after the match and bore the world senseless with stories of the ingenious ways in which your family dealt with standpipes in the 1976 drought. That was my generation's version of the spirit of the Blitz, and we weren't going to miss the chance of banging on about it.

I had chosen to turn up only just in time for the start, so that the Graduate could get on with it without my potentially confusing presence. The Tree Hugger had done the same, sauntering in to the changing room at five to six, as if not being in charge was the most natural thing in the world.

Two things became evident when I arrived. First, most White Hunters had turned up unusually early, when the norm was a perpetual race against the clock, and they were making it clear that their wisdom and seasoned advice was available to the

Graduate. Secondly, the Gun Runner's assertion of the lascivious goings on in the bedrooms of West Heath seemed to be based on a good deal of truth, and you could have cut the resulting atmosphere around their team with a knife.

'They look a cheerful lot,' commented the Sieve, on his way out to drop a few practice catches. We stood together and watched the Graduate and his cuckolded opposite number standing out in the middle for the toss, and were impressed that, from a distance at least, the Graduate appeared to be spelling out how it was going to be. He flicked the coin high in the air, looked down at it at once it had landed, and then made a muted batting action before shaking hands and walking back to the boundary.

'We're chasing,' he announced, and he asked the Engineer to go behind the stumps, immediately presenting himself with Leadership Challenge number one.

'So, you don't need me to keep, then?' asked the Sieve, much as a child would ask innocently for confirmation that the family Easter egg hunt had been cancelled.

'Let's see how we're going at ten overs,' said the Graduate, 'and we might swap. But I really want you for your speed on the cover boundary and don't want to waste you where you don't need to move.'

The Sieve thought about this for a moment, and in spite of its loose provenance, it seemed to satisfy him. To be wanted for a specific attribute on the cricket field was riches indeed if you were the Human Sieve, and he looked happy as he made his way to the fence in a manner calculated to denote athleticism.

As soon as he had passed Leadership Challenge number one, number two slid into view.

'I can't run, old boy,' said the Gun Runner. 'Put me in slip, would you.' He held his knee theatrically as if visualising the bullet that may or may not have scraped it in one of those early morning gunfights.

'I'm afraid I'm a bit crocked, too,' said the Tree Hugger, who had genuinely come off his bike the week before on the hairpin of an Italian mountainside, imagining himself to be twenty-five years younger, and fifty per cent more competitive, than he really was. 'Maybe put me in gully.'

'Me, too, I'm afraid,' added the Beekeeper. He didn't give a specific or verifiable reason, so the assumption had to be that he simply didn't fancy running around in the early evening heat. In fact, by the time the Graduate had looked around his team, there were only two players who were capable of being, or prepared to be, out on the boundary: the Young Farmer, because he was the best fielder, and the Sieve, because he had been flattered into thinking that prowling in the deep was what he had been put here on earth for.

'Can you go down to fine leg, please, Dad.' At a stroke he had solved the double problem of who to hide in the worst position, and how to cover behind the yet-to-be-truly-tested keeping of the Engineer, by dumping his father there. The move met with almost universal approval and he led the team out with something like a spring in his step. Besides, he had watched often enough over the years as I had done the same to the elderly, the infirm and the confused, and it was somehow comforting to know that the lessons had sunk in.

The Young Farmer was given the opening over, on the off-chance that he could get the cheap match ball to swing in whilst it still had some lacquer on it. It turned out that he could, and the batsman needed all his skill to keep it out.

'Shabash!' yelled the Gun Runner from slip.

The batsman looked quizzically at him, as if he had misheard, and then settled down to wait for the next ball. When it came, it kept straight, bypassing the bat and thumping into the Engineer's gloves with an encouraging thud.

'Ow!' squeaked the Engineer, wringing her right hand.

'Oh, shabash!' called the Gun Runner again, in an echo of games he had played in a different century on the dusty plains of Balochistan.

'Join the dots!' said the Sieve, his faint but cheerful voice drifting in from the boundary.

After half the overs had gone, the Tree Hugger started rotating and waving his arm in a way that looked as if he needed an urgent visit to the toilet, but which everyone present knew meant that he fancied a couple of overs himself.

'Can I just see how things go?', replied the Graduate, in a respectful echo of the Tree Hugger's own time-honoured brush-off line, when he didn't think the volunteer was up to it. The minute it was uttered, it was known by everyone on the pitch that, whoever else would have an over or two, it would definitely not be the Tree Hugger.

'Shabash!' said the Gun Runner, as if the whole thing had been part of a plan all along.

The general opinion was that the Graduate marshalled his troops pretty well during the opposition's innings, even if the circumstances had not been very challenging. Village teams come in two main shapes and sizes – the disconcertingly competitive league version, and its opposite number, which looks as if it has been put together haphazardly in the pub the night before – and there was no doubt to which group this one belonged.

Normally such a team would make up in geniality what they were missing in competence, but West Heath, with their unfortunate off-field intrigue, appeared to have about six different elephants hiding behind bits of furniture in their room, and occasionally one would escape. They were a nice bunch, but they were slowly being torn apart by the insistence of both keeper and skipper to keep turning up for each and every match.

They scored 105 for eight in their twenty overs, which the Graduate told us was 'gettable', but only if we 'put our heads down'. He created a batting order that satisfied most people and then called over to me:

'I'd like you at eleven, please,' he said with a mischievous smile, 'to give some stability and leadership to the tail.'

In an exhibition of the triumph of nurture over nature, the little sod was parroting back every trick of the trade he had heard me deploy these last eight or so years, and it was hard not to admire a bit of it. The whole place was alive with the sound of chickens flapping lazily in to roost, and I was hoping that he wouldn't remember the old chestnut of putting lower-order batsmen straight out into the field to umpire, rather than leaving them to enjoy the keg of beer that had made its way to the boundary's edge now that the opposition were in the field. Making myself scarce for a minute or two would do the trick, and I started to head off to the changing room.

'Oh, and numbers ten and eleven,' he called after me. 'Would you mind umpiring for a bit?'

And without pausing for a second glance, he marched off towards the scorebook to fill in the batting order. There were no ruses that he didn't know and couldn't use. Imitation is the sincerest form of flattery, and didn't he know it.

So out we went, each in our white coats and with our six pieces of gravel, and we settled ourselves to watch what we fondly believed would be a progression to victory. However, West Heath might have been pretty useless corporately, but they had a secret weapon in the form of a young lad who had recently been turned down for the role of opening bowler for the Hampshire

Under 18s, and he had lots of residual energy and a serious grudge to make good.

Of the many things that the Graduate had remembered to negotiate at the beginning of the match, unfortunately limiting the number of overs per bowler wasn't one, so the sad fact was that a near County player with a point to prove was going to chuck down exactly half of the twenty overs we were due to receive. Fast bowlers are expected to look angry and determined, whereas this one merely seemed bored, and very slightly disappointed.

Appearances can be deceptive and the fact that he wore thick John Lennon glasses at the top end of his body, and loose trousers that kept falling halfway down his buttocks at the bottom end, hid from us momentarily that he was in a class of his own. In the old days, a man could at least rely on quick bowlers to look the part.

By the end of the first over, we were two for two, and by the end of the third we had progressed to five for four, with every decent bat we had back in the hutch. An experienced cricketer comes to know when a crisis is tapping at the window by the sudden rush to replace umpires with dismissed batsmen, which was exactly what happened to the Gun Runner and me within a mere quarter of an hour of heading off out into the middle.

Suddenly, we were padded up and sitting on the bench by the wooden scoreboard, watching our innings disintegrate, and wondering what we would be able to do about it ourselves. The eighth wicket went down at 60, and the ninth two balls later at the same score, leaving one wicket for them to get and forty-six highly unlikely runs for us to score. For the second time in a week, the Beekeeper and I found ourselves out in the middle together, but this time round things didn't look quite so clever.

'Got any ideas?' I asked him during our first mid-wicket conference.

I thought briefly of all the coaching I had done back in the spring, and of those long-ago sessions with the sports psychologist, and I knew instinctively what both would say. The coach would tell me to play the ball in the way I had been taught, and not to play the situation. And the psychologist would tell me to treat it all as a challenge, and not as a threat, and to enjoy it. 'Am I being a good coach to myself?' she would want me to ask.

'Not really,' he replied. 'It's all a bit shit.'

But he reminded me that we had extracted sixty-five jars of honey from our hive only two days ago, and that life was looking up. Men who could show that kind of talent at their hives could probably replicate it anywhere.

But opportunities, as Sun Tzu never tired of pointing out, multiply as they are seized, and sometimes, just sometimes, we see people make the same mistakes as we routinely make ourselves. Maybe West Heath's skipper had other things on his mind, possibly the likely geographic whereabouts of his wife in about three hours' time, but he suddenly decided to take the Hampshire youth player off for the fifteenth over, and to bowl it himself, with the effect that his only over cost seventeen runs. The next over went for twelve, which left us nineteen to get off the last three, and by the start of the last over, with the Beekeeper facing, we had nine to score. Ominously, it was due to be bowled by the youngster.

Keeping me off strike seemed to be a workable and laudable tactic, at least it was as far as I was concerned, and for the first four balls it worked. Then, unaccountably, he called me through for a quick single off the fifth ball, leaving me to take a minimum of four off the last one. We don't often go down to the wire, and this called for a further mid-wicket conference.

'What's he going to bowl, do you reckon?' I asked the Beekeeper.

'Something on your toes. Just take a swing. Do it for the bees. And don't cock it up.'

Three decades of cricket persuaded me, however, that he would fire it at yorker length, as far outside the offside as he could without it being called a wide, but still well beyond the realistic capabilities of someone like me to do anything useful to it. It really didn't matter what he bowled, to be honest, as I had long since decided what shot I would play, and where I would be standing when I played it.

Probably something in my demeanour unsettled his adolescent composure, and when he finally sent the ball down after a seemingly endless pause for discussion with his skipper, it was indeed outside the off stump, but it was coming through at about waist height, which was where my premeditated shot was starting its short, circular life.

Coaching or no coaching, I knew only too well the shot that had got me most of my 4,500 runs over the years, and I wasn't about to try anything fancy. The bat came through and caught the thickest of outside edges, which propelled the ball high over the two slips and down to the boundary for four. We had won the squeakiest of narrow victories off the last ball.

'Shabash!' came a loud voice from the boundary.

Sport is made up of many dreams, some pure, some recycled. It has to be this way, otherwise we wouldn't do it.

Equally, memory tends to project past things as an exaggerated form of how they actually happened, with the bad getting worse and the good growing steadily better. So it was that hours later, in two separate bedrooms in the same house back in West Sussex, a young club captain turned his bedside light off and recalled to his own profound satisfaction the various bits of tactical genius with which he had engineered a victory out of nothing.

Meanwhile, one floor below, a number eleven batsman purred in pleasure at the memory of the dreamy cover drive that had flowed all the way along the ground from his bat to the point boundary to seal the victory.

9 When the Rains Came

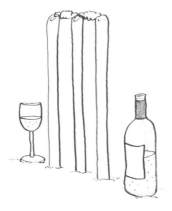

Late August

THE high pressure had finally moved away from the Azores. All summer long, it had been the benign influence on our season and had brought us unbroken sunshine and warmth. Now that it was weakening, it was allowing the build-up of hurricanes out in the Caribbean, which in turn brought the chastening weather systems that soaked our grounds, and inconvenienced my bees.

These days, team captains arm themselves with rain-prediction apps that help them decide whether play is likely on a certain day, and when to press the go/no-go button. Moving images of how the rain-bearing clouds have moved in the last four hours combine with the more general weather forecasts to give an accurate enough picture to prevent people setting off on long, fruitless journeys.

The Breeder comes into his own at times like this, as his very livelihood depends on making the right call, week in, week out. If we are lucky, the Gun Runner furnishes us with top secret satellite imagery from a contact at the CIA, a treat that would be even better if anyone had the faintest idea of how to interpret it.

Psychologically, though, the later in the season you find yourself, the rarity value of each remaining fixture makes the cancellation decision progressively harder. Sometimes it is done for you by the groundsman or opposition skipper, who has been out at 6.00 a.m., staring down at a waterlogged square from under the shadow of an umbrella; at other times, the grim weather is all the fig leaf required to let a team off the hook when they have only nine players in the first place, and one of those is an eight-year-old girl, who volunteered solely because, for the first and last time, she can't get enough of being with her father this summer. Either way, summer rain feels much wetter and colder to a cricketer than the stuff that comes down in December.

Like the ageing process, rain is deeply ingrained in the cricketer's psyche, the yin to the yang of his bright sunshine. In the gallery of our mind's eye, we tend to see cricket as a series of Ravilious watercolours, all dappled sunlight, ice cream and green grass, and, ideally, dampness has no part in it. At one extreme of reality, however, lies the certainties of a long, hot summer, where even the most Eeyore-like player doesn't bother with checking the weather forecasts, and at the other end, the absoluteness of a tropical downpour that brings all outside life to an end.

These we can normally handle. It is the will-it-wont-it vagaries of our climate that do the most damage to our morale, where the weekend forecast changes each day of the preceding week and it is impossible to say with any conviction if the game will go ahead or not. We play this game because we love it, and that is why we mind much more than adults should when our hopes are dashed, raised and dashed again.

We are an homogenous tribe, and you can recognise us as we stand around in shorts anywhere in these islands of ours on a Saturday lunchtime, in small groups on wet outfields, ground water lapping over the soles of our sandals, and the faint sound of air being sucked through teeth.

Our last southern match of this year was on a wet, late-August Saturday, on a hillside Wealden ground, which is featured frequently on the front cover of one of those magazines you only ever find in a dentist's waiting room. The Tree Hugger emailed his thoughts late the evening before:

Can't really cancel as it hasn't rained yet, but forecast very dodgy. Plus, we've probably got the best team we've had out this season. Anyway, opposition have lost contact details of the groundsman, and hopefully he has lost theirs. Besides, I've got four bloody sliced loaves for the tea, and a pig's worth of ham. Let's do it.

And then, a few minutes later:

Who's got the scorebook?

Recruitment problems at this stage of the season are less significant than in earlier months. The younger members are back from their travels, but not yet back at university freshers' weeks, playing truth or dare with their livers, and the older players just want to get as many games in before the seven-month lay-off, possibly in case vital bits of them erode away or perish in the close season, and prevent them from taking to the field again.

The Gun Runner, taking a short break from his day job in the war-torn hinterlands of Juba, couldn't get enough of us, and had gone so far as to commit to the French tour at the end of the month. He had even thrown in a spontaneous 'shabash' when I had asked him along, and explained that he could probably recruit a couple of members of the French Foreign Legion down there if we were short. The Breeder had already brought his harvest home, which in his case happens to be bull's semen heading into the test tube, and he had down time, too.

The Engineer had liked enough of what she had seen of us over her first few matches, and had more or less thrown her lot in with us permanently. Our hope at this stage was that she would act as a kind of contented tethered goat, and eventually attract more women into the club; as close as we had come to a diversity policy since recruiting the Human Sieve a decade before. Throw in a few youngsters, the Wealth Manager, Tree Hugger and a Beekeeper or two, and the match was fully subscribed without the need for even one begging or threatening email.

SOMETIMES I think we only do it for the grounds we go to.

After thirty-three years of existence, our club is closing in on its one hundredth different venue. Back in the early days, we would go anywhere that would have us: if you had offered us a game on a desolate, windblown patch of earth hard by a nuclear reprocessing plant back then, we would have bitten your hand off for it, and volunteered to provide the tea and to throw in our bank details into the bargain.

But, over the years, and by degrees, our priorities changed and we hunted for pitches whose beauty took our breath away when we first saw them, and whose aesthetics could mop away the hours of failure we were often fated to provide when on them. It felt occasionally that we were trying to be the physical embodiment of a Merchant Ivory film, minus the floppy hair, and the Edwardian homoeroticism. Possibly minus Dame Maggie Smith, as well, but I wouldn't like to say.

Over each winter, the Tree Hugger and I would log down the perfect pitches that we happened to spot from footpaths, from our cars, from trains, even from planes, as we went about our normal business, and then we would start the insidious process of sidling up digitally to the resident team there, and flattering them into giving us a fixture, in return for one the following year at ours. We probably acquired a reputation for being a bit hard to please, but we could never have been faulted for our gratitude once we got there.

For the last match of August, we had hired the pitch at Elsted, a tiny downland village that straddles a ridge in West Sussex, and which possesses the four prerequisites of a fine ground: great view, character, a true wicket and an unpretentious pub nearby. And it was into this unpretentious pub that we now found ourselves running through the horizontal rain about an hour before the match was due to start, and it was inside it, to our joy and astonishment, that we rediscovered the Poet.

'I thought you might need an umpire,' he said.

FOR many years, the Poet had been a stalwart of the club, and the de facto custodian of any cultural values to which it might lay claim. Whilst the remaining ten of us would get on with the mundane business of organising and playing competitive cricket, the Poet would lurk somewhere near the boundary's edge, ignoring the game, charming all around him, and availing himself of a wide variety of stimulants that appeared to have come either from the local off-licence, or from a bearded bloke round the back of the Petersfield Leisure Centre.

His batting and fielding were awful, but his bowling was curiously effective, line-and-length stuff and, until his automotive system started to feel the strain of the years that he had put it through, he was among our most reliable wicket takers. Like the Ginger, he never appealed, believing that to do so was to be unacceptably attention-seeking, but instead he would engage the umpire in polite, philosophical conversation, at some point of which he would, or might, raise the tiny matter of the merits of the previous ball.

A few years ago, he had turned up for a match one day and simply announced it to be his last, and for a time we worried that there might be something seriously wrong with his health that had led to this decision. So to see him sitting, pint in hand, at the Three Horseshoes, was a pleasure indeed, and we immediately accepted his offer to help officiate the coming match; a prospect that was becoming fainter by the minute, on account of the driving curtains of rain that were sweeping in from the Downs, and lashing belts of wetness against the steamed-up windows of the pub.

Had it not been the last match, we would have cancelled long before now. As it was, it was clear to even the most optimistic of us that the game wasn't going to happen, despite the forecast of bright sunshine for large parts of the afternoon after 3.00 p.m.: the ground would be too waterlogged.

This feeling was confirmed by the arrival in the public bar of the soaked groundsman, just before our sandwiches arrived, and it meant that, once we had contacted the opposition captain and the residue of our players, at least we could settle in for the afternoon. The caveat to all this was hidden in the phrase 'once we had contacted', which did not take into account the vagaries of mobile coverage in the weald of Sussex.

There are some definite features of team communication in the digital age that we have assimilated over the years, which, if we *had* standard procedures, we would have built into them.

Ten golden rules for cricket communication in the digital age

1. There is no signal at any cricket ground in the UK. Or, if there is, there won't be when you need it.

2. You can only communicate with someone below the age of twenty-five via an App that you have never heard of, and which will be obsolete in nine months.

3. You can only communicate with someone above the age of sixty by landline or Royal Mail. However, if you call said landline, no one will answer it, because no one ever does, other than the Granny who comes to stay at Christmas.

4. No one over the age of fifty remembers to charge their phone, which means that, even if they had one, and even if it had a signal, it wouldn't be working anyway.

5. Equally, no one over the age of fifty, and with a functioning brain, reads tweets and, far less, writes them.

6. The player who is about to let you down because his circumstances have mysteriously 'changed' on the morning

of the match will do so by text, and will then unaccountably lose signal for the rest of the afternoon, possibly the rest of his life.

7. You are expected to know by telepathy which of their work or home email addresses each player would like you to communicate with them on, even when they change preferences every week or so.

8. The postcode that the opposition skipper gave you will take your Satnav, your car and you to an industrial estate four and half miles from the ground you are trying to get to, with a large and grid-locked town in between you and it.

9. If in doubt, they didn't hear, or weren't listening anyway, and you can rely on the fact that they won't do the logical thing in default of a call from you.

10. The player who is captured on film executing an exquisite cover drive will suddenly, and inexplicably, abandon a lifetime's contempt of people who post things on Facebook, and will post the image on Facebook with a suitably faux-modest comment.

On top of all this, the Gun Runner still uses cleft sticks and old tribal smoke signals. His phone has long since been confiscated by Sudanese intelligence, and his email account has probably been hacked by Edward Snowden.

'WHAT are we to do?' exclaimed the Poet slightly theatrically, after a mere handful of pints. 'Here we all are, like a bridesmaid with no wedding to go to. We need an activity.' And he was right. We live and operate in a maritime, temperate climate, where rain is a frequent intruder into our cricket, and yet all we ever think about, talk about, write about, is sunshine and long shadows on the baked, parched grass. We would have played around a hundred matches more than we actually have over the last thirty years if it didn't rain so frequently, and the Poet was simply articulating the need to profit from the unscheduled free time.

The rain had abated in the hour that we had been in the pub, by which time the Gun Runner had offered us a dozen war stories, and the sun was showing up through the half-steamed up window as a faint luminous disc in a watery, grey sky. The Tree Hugger suggested go-karting down at Gosport, until he was reminded that it cost about £30 a head, and that this represented a fortnight of food for an undergraduate, a couple of large hay bales for the Breeder, and God knows what for the Poet.

It being a Saturday, and the pub being open all day and relatively comfortable, the Graduate came up with the idea of an early doors lock in; it gained a certain amount of traction, but not enough to swing it. In the end, it was the Beekeeper's suggestion that we repaired to the nearby Petersfield 'pay-and-play' golf course, and saw what happened when we tried our hands at a different sport. After all, we were not expected back to our various homes before early evening.

The rain had swept back in as the eight of us turned up at the pay-and-play about a quarter of an hour later, paid our £12 green fee, and assembled on the first tee. Two of the team hadn't made it to the pub in the first place, and the Young Farmer, declaring golf to be a still-ball sport that was 'dead from the neck up', had headed home.

The Poet had announced that his current religion forbade him to take part in competitive sports these days, and in consequence, he would follow us around and keep the score, but not before he had slipped a couple of cans of Guinness and a strange-looking packet into a pocket of my bag.

'Emergency supplies,' he said conspiratorially. That left six of us to make up two threesomes, and plough our way through the dankness of a September afternoon.

Cricket and golf are similar in the sense that they provide simultaneously for internal, individual and team battles, all wrapped up in one envelope. For a batsman, however, they offer the additional luxury of every shot not threatening to be the last; indeed, the worse you are, the more shots you get, and the more shots you take, the more value you extract from your green fee.

On this basis, the Engineer and the Sieve recouped their £12.00 many times over, and, as the afternoon wore on, each player revealed themselves to play golf very much in the style that they played cricket. The Beekeeper with powerful elegance, the Tree Hugger with fussy detail, and the Graduate with homicidal brutality. The Ginger, as with his other sport, basically had but the one shot, and he altered it only in terms of the power needed to get the ball the distance it needed to go. And, wherever you happened to be as the game progressed, the loud voice of the Gun Runner marshalling his troops and exhorting us all to greater efforts would boom out around the birch trees and bullrushes.

By the end of the round, none of it mattered, as no one apart from the Tree Hugger had kept their score.

BACK in the pub afterwards, the Poet waxed lyrical about the mateship that he had so missed since he had packed in playing.

'It's like our "American Pie",' he announced, in homage to Don McLean's voice filtering out of the speaker system behind the bar.

The Graduate, who loved 'American Pie' almost as much as he loved Fulham Football Club, asked him to explain.

'Well, it was a lyrical picture of small-town America in 1959 after the air crash that killed Buddy Holly. Until the song got murdered by Madonna thirty years later, it was the definitive joining of dots of the zeitgeist of that place, at that time.'

The Beekeeper, for whom zeitgeist was an entirely alien notion and more likely to be a type of German brassica than a sociological term, was about to comment, but then understood that the Poet was happily off on one of his famous monologues. It was best to leave him burbling on as, over the years, some of our finest moments had been spent listening to him going off on one, and wondering where on earth it would all lead, and how it might end.

After a further five minutes, during which he touched on all the theoretical meanings of all the allusions in the song, tortuously managing to connect them back to the cricket we all played together, he suddenly found he had no more to give.

'It's *our* "American Pie",' he repeated with finality. 'Only English.'

He paused, gazing up at a cheap hunting print on the wall of the bar. 'Perhaps it's our English Spotted Dick.' And off he went again.

Outside in the wet streets, the rain had set in for the evening. Whereas, I was sitting in a pub, laughing so much it almost hurt, and I still had Staffordshire, the librarians, and France to come.

10 *Alstonefield*

Early September

MANY years ago, the Graduate kicked the great Sir Garfield Sobers in the small of the back.

Granted, the Graduate was only three years old at the time, and the West Indian all-rounder was occupying the seat immediately in front of him on a night flight across the Atlantic, but a kick is a kick, and in consequence, an apology needed to be an apology.

When I saw who it was, I became almost comically starstruck, servile even. 'So very sorry,' I seemed to hear myself saying, 'almost anyone else wouldn't have mattered, but you! You with the six sixes in an over off Malcolm Nash; you with your 365 against Pakistan all those years ago; you with the first knighthood for Caribbean sport! Just say the word and I shall have him put in the hold with the luggage. He will be deprived entry to the UK tomorrow morning, or locked in the toilet for the rest of the flight.'

But Sobers just smiled at me, saying that it was of small consequence, and his wife could sit there from now on. 'She is a good sleeper, you see,' he said reassuringly.

Twenty years later, how I wish that I had taken that bullet myself instead of his wife. She could have sat next to the Graduate in the row behind, delighting in his interesting repertoire of dinosaur jokes and stories, and I could have filled the next six hours sitting next to the great man and putting the world of cricket to rights.

Eventually, that conversation would have turned to captaincy, his of the West Indies, and mine of the White Hunters, and at some point, I would have said, 'Now tell me, Sir Garfield, what was the most bizarre reason you had for not having your two opening bowlers available for the first two overs of a Test match?'

And, whatever else would have deprived him of the services of Messrs Hall and Griffith, it wouldn't have been that Wes Hall's vintage MG Roadster had broken down four miles from the pitch outside a Derbyshire housing estate, and that Charlie Griffith decided it would be nice to wait with him there in the sunshine for the AA to come and sort it out; never mind that the AA said they couldn't be there until forty minutes after the match was starting.

That dubious honour came nearly forty years later, and from the Breeder and his son.

It wasn't the perfect start to our much-anticipated revenge

match against Alstonefield Cricket Club, 200 miles to the north of our normal stamping grounds, but it was in keeping with the way we did things.

Over the years, a list has evolved of the main differences between the work of a Test captain and a White Hunter one, which goes something like this:

- THE Test captain is normally accompanied on to the field by ten players. It would be unusual for one to be on the loo and one still on the A34 as the rest of the team took to the field.

- THE Test captain doesn't suddenly run back to the pavilion to agree with his opposite number the interpretation of the lbw rule, the 'retire at fifty' convention, and exactly what time to put the tea urn on.

- IT is not normal practice for the Test captain to have to promise his strike bowler an extra two overs providing he agrees to bat at eleven …

- … neither does he have to put someone in at the top of the batting order simply because they are going out to supper in Marlborough and need to be away by 5.30 at the absolute latest, otherwise their wife will strangle them.

- HE very rarely has to call a halt to a bowler's over halfway through, on the basis that it is so bad, and so full of wides and no balls, that darkness is likely to fall before he completes it.

- HE doesn't have to hide his three worst fielders in positions of no consequence ...

- ... or agree that the wicket-keepers will swap gloves at the halfway stage, otherwise, he won't have enough bowlers to do the full number of overs.

- HE doesn't have to wonder if that new bloke who came along at the last minute with the Wealth Manager is a proper cricketer (who should bat early and bowl often), or a friend from the Marketing Department who only came along for some fresh air, and had borrowed some kit off his son.

- HE doesn't have to ask the opposition skipper if he can borrow a couple of fielders to cover for the two of his own who haven't turned up, and are out of phone contact.

- AND finally, he doesn't have to ask his opposite number to put a slow underarm bowler on for the last over, so that his wicket-keeper's ten-year-old son can have a safe and meaningful bat without having his block knocked off by a deranged psychopath.

Sobers, Richards, Ponting and Root. They don't know they're bloody born. They have selection committees, well-rewarded players and a whole backroom of staff who tell them how to play, think and even eat properly. We, on the other hand, have the Tree Hugger and me frantically emailing anyone with a functioning pulse once a week, begging them to forgo their afternoon's gardening to come and play cricket with us.

Also, I'll bet none of them have ever had to ask the opposition skipper to play the 'not out first ball' rule.

By this late stage of the season, the White Hunters were as close as they ever tended to come to being on a roll. A small roll, maybe, and only a half-baked one filled with pallid sausage meat of the sort that you might find in a cheap bakery chain the one time you are early for an appointment, but it was a roll nonetheless. Where we came from in the sporting firmament, that was riches indeed. We weren't exactly getting cocky, but it would be fair to say that the cockerel within us was stirring.

Players who would habitually dwell in mediocrity behind the battlements were suddenly sticking their heads above the parapet and making contributions of consequence. Granted, we were not quite at that cup winners' stage, where teams jump up and down annoyingly for the cameras on a raised dais in front of the sponsor's logo, spraying champagne and confetti over all and sundry, but we were improving.

We knew that we were getting better, if only because the Sieve had started to take two out of three balls cleanly of late, and the Engineer had nearly taken a couple at slip.

Personally, I had abandoned my 'new me' plans almost completely, and was motivated more by the joy of being there at all than by any idea that I could improve by going back to basics. One of the hardest tricks with a social cricket side, where participants change from week to week, is to achieve a consistent sense of progress and belonging; however, at this stage of the season we had boiled down to a hard core of thirteen or fourteen players, and we were beginning to feel like a team. Even the meanest among us were getting wallets out without the heavy-lifting gear needing to be deployed.

As we entered September, we had four matches left, counting the French tour, which wasn't for another month, anyway. One was our match against the Librarians but, before that, we were returning to the small Staffordshire village of Alstonefield, to rekindle a relationship with the club and their ground that had first delighted us a few years ago.

Originally slated to be part of a long weekend tour in the area, before we organised our trip to France, we had stuck with the distant match as a one-off, because our hosts were friends, and we wanted to keep the fixture alive for future years. The plan was to go up and back in thirty-six hours and make the very best of it. After all, finding a congenial, non-league, village side that wants you back is worth more than gold, and a match in September is worth double one in July.

We were helped or hindered, depending on which way you looked at it, by various component members of the team being on experimental phases in parts of their lives. Late seasons are like that: people get carried away.

The Graduate, having been right-handed from birth, suddenly decided that he was born to be a left-hander, and changed sides overnight, accordingly. The theory among his teammates was that a late-night's binge-watching of Ben Stokes's 258 at Cape Town in 2016 on YouTube had got amongst him, and he had developed the curious notion that the full panoply of Stokes's shots could only be his if he emulated everything else as well.

As if that wasn't enough, the Tree Hugger had conjured up a disguised slower ball, never mind that it was almost impossible to go slower than the ball he bowled already, and he was determined to bring it to the light of day among the peaks and dry-stone walls of north-east Staffordshire.

Finally, the Wealth Manager had recalibrated his body clock and decided to pitch up on time for each game if he possibly could, even if that meant needing to have an extra couple of pints at the pub before any given match, a personal sacrifice typical of the man and the team he represented. These were changes that were testament to man's extraordinary ability to adapt to the changing environment around them, but they also tended to turn captaincy into a blind exercise of hope versus experience.

The previous night, pitiful economic refugees from the Home Counties that we were, we had discovered by chance that a tenner could comfortably get in a round of pints and shorts for the entire team in the British Legion in Hartington, and we were not quite at our enthusiastic and competitive best when the remains of us were washed up at the Alstonefield ground at lunch-time the following day.

One thing had led to another at the Legion, as it had done the previous year, and every time it seemed the right moment to head back to the pub we were staying in, another White Hunter would discover an opportunity to buy the cheapest round of their lives, and would insist that they were allowed to exhibit their latent generosity before we turned in.

'No, no! I insist,' the Beekeeper had said, rather too theatrically, as the moths circled up and out of his wallet. 'Let me treat you all.'

'Surely it's my round,' said the Sieve, who had certainly never used those last two words in that particular order in the previous couple of decades.

'Absolutely not,' exclaimed the Tree Hugger, used to the punishing prices of drinks in the city of Winchester. 'This one's on me, for sure.'

The Engineer, in contrast, whose wallet had been generously deployed throughout her first season, couldn't get a look in. Cheap drink does something strange to cricket teams, and the prices in the Legion basically demanded eleven rounds from the eleven players.

And on and on it went, with the bar staff happy to prime the pump every twenty minutes or so, and the hard-core tourists drifting dangerously downwards into a world of spinning pillows and sickeningly winking fried eggs at the reluctant breakfast table.

'No need to toss,' said the Alstonefield skipper, what seemed a miserably short few hours later. 'What would you like to do?'

Over the years, we have rather liked losing the toss, as it takes the immediate responsibility away, and gives us something tangible to blame if it all goes wrong. Deciding what to do if and when we win the toss becomes a team debate, sometimes even a vote. Democracy and dictatorship snuggle easily together in the White Hunter Cricket Club, as do indecision and spontaneity.

We have played together so much over the years that we can watch the body language of the skipper out in the middle and know immediately from the hieroglyphics of his actions not only whether he has won the toss, but also what we will be doing in consequence. On a number of occasions, the Tree Hugger has even pretended to the team that he has lost a toss, to quash any idea that his decision might be to blame for the subsequent defeat.

The skipper's invitation came before we had fully grasped that thirty per cent of our bowling attack was still in some lay-by in Ashbourne, eating Mini Cheddars and waiting for the AA, so the Tree Hugger said that we would chase.

Gathering the troops entailed the usual time-consuming routines that it always seemed to do: dragging the Beekeeper away from the online reportage of another pitiful Norwich defeat; parting the Ginger and the Wealth Manager, who occupied diametrically opposite ends of the political spectrum, from a potentially heated discussion about government grants for wind turbines; and reassuring the Graduate that, yes, he could have a bowl when the ball 'still had some shine on it'.

Ten minutes later, we were out in the middle with two substitute fielders, and the Young Farmer pawing at the ground at the end of his run-up.

Behind him in the middle distance were the blue-green dales of the Peak District, and the sound of dog barking at dog from the isolation of a dozen sheep farms in the valley below us. There was soft music coming from an adjacent campsite, and a sky-full of buzzards were circling high above us. For a time, it was impossible to think that we were here for sport, and not the view.

The Young Farmer produced five quick and accurate inswinging deliveries, which were blocked out respectfully by the opening bat. The sixth gave a bit more width and he cut at it, a shot he probably wouldn't have played if he had allowed for the extra bounce the long, dry spell had given the already free-draining wicket. He got a thin but audible deflection, which went through as a well-taken catch by the Wealth Manager, who was substituting as wicket-keeper for the crocked Sieve.

It was as unassuming a show of competence as we had managed all season, and we duly clustered round the Wealth Manager and Young Farmer to tell them so. Cricket teams that had passages of play like this had a funny old habit of becoming cricket teams that went on to win matches. We weren't there yet, of course, but we had started well.

And well is how it carried on through the early afternoon. Emerging out of its collective hangover, like explorers blinking their wonderment on reaching the tropical beach after months in the rain forest, the White Hunters kept things surprisingly tight. Apart from a sharp drop at slip by the skipper, we fielded most things cleanly, and took the catches offered us as if routine.

'We're quite excited about this match,' said one of the late-order incoming batsmen. 'For the first time in our history, we've gone unbeaten throughout the season. This is our last match, and it's why we've put together the strongest team we can.'

If he had told us this early on, we would probably have done our normal thing, and worried ourselves into being as bad as the formbook suggested we should be. A fear of heights would have got to us again, and events would have unfolded along their normal mediocre sequence.

But there was only one batsman in after him, and the damage to their team had already been done. Wickets had been shared between the Young Farmer, the Graduate, and the two Breeders, once the AA had done a quick patch-up job on the MG's failed oil seal.

With four overs left, the Tree Hugger started turning his arm over in a manner seeming to suggest that he was going to try out his experimental ball before the innings closed and, at 155 for eight, it seemed churlish for him not to give himself an over. We duly scattered to the four corners, each one doing his personal calculation of how many runs we could afford to give away if the over slipped from his control, and into chaos. We needn't have worried.

Ball number one was, indeed, slower than anything we had ever seen him bowl. Here, somewhere beyond the start of his seventh decade, we watched the Tree Hugger trundle down the runway of his unfeasibly long run-up, tongue hanging out and right arm hanging down, like Bob Willis used to do.

Then, when he got to his delivery stride, he seemed to suspend forward motion entirely, and eventually catapult the ball out of the back of his right hand in a perfectly straight line down the pitch. A memory stirred within me that this was how we had been taught as young soldiers to lob grenades into nearby block houses.

The batsman, who had enough time to do most of his weekend online shopping in the period it took the ball to travel those twenty-two yards, made an entirely justifiable decision to take two paces down the wicket and blast the ball back over the bowler's head, over the dry-stone wall, and down towards those barking sheepdogs in the valley below.

But suddenly the ball dipped on him when the kinetic energy ran dry, turned ever so slightly to the off, and passed his bat by the best part of three inches. With the batsman stranded about five yards down the track, it was the work of a second for the Wealth Manager to take the bails off and go up for an entirely unnecessary appeal. Substitute keeper he might have been, and nursing a weapons-grade hangover as he definitely was, there was no way on earth he was going to miss an opportunity like this.

The difference between the Young Farmer, say, and the Tree Hugger, as the novelist E. W. Howe once said, is that 'a young man is a theory, but an old man is a fact'. This made the result of the Tree Hugger's quiet theorising all the more magnificent. It wasn't any old wicket; this was one that had been born in the armchair of his sitting room, cradled in his car on the way up and then forged in the gentle heat of our battle with Alstonefield, and it had worked perfectly. There is nothing like the quiet joy of an old amateur sportsman, who has not only predicted what he is going to do, but then achieved it. Age has plenty of lows, but they generally serve to make the highs even higher.

'It was probably crap,' he said, with the air of a man who clearly thought it wasn't, and rather wanted ten voices to argue its brilliance all the more energetically. None did.

'Yup,' said the Beekeeper. 'But crap balls take wickets.'

'Not crap,' said the Young Farmer. 'But very, very close to it.'

'Oh, well bowled!' said the Breeder.

Deflated ever so slightly, he went back to his mark to bowl, if it was possible, an even slower delivery, even further out of the back of his hand, and looped up even higher into the autumn sky. The number eleven bat, more used to being peppered by angry league bowlers trying to finish things off quickly, came skipping down the wicket, like a spring cow to its pasture, and made the softest of connections straight back into the Tree Hugger's outstretched hands.

His analysis read: 0.2–0–0–2, and Alstonefield were all out for 155.

'Still crap,' said the Beekeeper. 'But strangely effective.'

'That's great bowling,' added the Breeder, still incapable of grasping the irony of the Tree Hugger having had two monumentally lucky breaks. Geniality is a hard habit to break.

THE Gun Runner was on the phone to Afghanistan when we were sorting out the batting order. The idea had been to let him open the innings, as he had been harbouring this deep, and entirely correct, suspicion that we only ever put him in at nine, ten or eleven.

'I'm better than that, you know,' he had said cheerfully, as he piled into the last of the Bakewell tarts. Then he had gone off to a quiet spot to discuss the security situation in Jellalabad, with a man who used to be in the mujahideen, but now sold himself alternately to the highest bidder.

'I told you *pomegranate* is just a code word!' we heard him shout down the phone. 'You can't really have thought that I actually bloody wanted eight hundred kilos of pomegranates. I mean, what do you think I actually do for a living?'

As a rule, people's work calls during cricket matches are, at best, a nuisance and at worst, a blatant intrusion. Granted, occasionally you hear the Breeder having to redirect half a litre of Red Devon semen to some distant ranch, or the Wealth Manager fielding a panic call from a client who realises that he has slipped four places to 198th in the *Sunday Times* Rich List but, by and large, we leave our phones in our cars.

But there was something rakish and adventurous about the Gun Runner's shouting match with his Afghan contact, and gradually both teams were sidling up to him, and egging him on to even greater efforts.

'You're opening,' said the Tree Hugger casually, as a stream of Pashtun invective was coming down at him over the phone. The Gun Runner winked, and gave him the thumbs up to ensure that the message had been received, and that the place wasn't to be offered to anyone else.

'I have to go, Ahmadullah,' he said. 'The security situation where I am has just got significantly worse.' At which point he went off to find some pads and a bat from the club kit, leaving the rest of us lost in admiration, out there in the war-torn hell of the Staffordshire Peaks.

Out they went, Gun Runner and Graduate, each one simultaneously student and master to the other, with one explaining how to deal with the rising ball, and the other talking about the glorious potential ahead of them.

Social cricket is the ultimate sport of self-regulation, in that the officials normally come from the side that is batting, and not from a pool of neutrals, who actually know what they are talking about. Most White Hunters rule themselves out of umpiring through ignorance, incompetence, idleness, or a combination of all three. So it is the privilege of a select few of us to take our turn behind the stumps, and try to keep count of the number of balls and, when required, reach the correct decisions on thin edges, run outs and – above all – lbws.

Morally, we tend to be up to it, which is more than can be said for some of the teams we have played over the years. Ninety per cent of the decisions are self-sorting, providing that you follow the basic pitch-impact-wicket principles, and it is only on the margins that judgment is required.

The first ball was due to be bowled at the Gun Runner, and I was the standing umpire at the bowler's end. It was quickish, full, and it thumped into his front pad.

'How's that?' asked the bowler and keeper in unison.

'Not out,' I said. 'Going down leg,' which it sort of was. It was one of those marginal ones that isn't embarrassing not to give 'out', especially not on the first ball, but could just as easily go the other way. He looked at me thoughtfully, and went back to his mark.

The second ball thudded into his pad as well, and an even louder appeal emerged, this time from the whole team. I looked up at the Gun Runner's face, on which was written a mixture of defiance and pitiful pleading.

'Not out,' I said. 'A little bit high,' which, again, it sort of was. At this point, the Gun Runner was in a version of Schrödinger's cat paradox, in that he was neither provably dead nor provably alive in cricketing terms. He had been the beneficiary of two close calls which, aggregated, meant that any reasonable shout in future would have him. It shouldn't be this way, but it is.

The third ball also thumped into his pad, but not before it had taken a small deflection off the bat. It was the first one that was palpably not out and I couldn't, in any conscience, give it.

To my relief, the bowler, who was both an experienced and sporting player, let me off the hook. 'Inside edge?' he suggested, and I agreed.

By now, the Gun Runner had metamorphosed from the brash confident buccaneer of only a few minutes ago into a gibbering wreck. He went for a stroll towards the square leg umpire to collect his thoughts, and then readied himself again. The fourth ball duly smacked into his front pad and my finger went straight up.

Unfortunately, it went straight up before the bowler had even appealed, which made the long drive south with the Gun Runner three hours later an interesting one. It didn't help either that the bowler said, 'Are you sure?', in the earshot of the departing batsman.

It was meant as an ironic comment on the three previous appeals that had been turned down, but the Gun Runner took it to mean that he had been the victim of an intense miscarriage of justice, and he would now brood on it all winter. Ahmadullah and his pomegranates receded briefly into the background as the biggest problem of his afternoon.

The next over consisted of our new left-hander, in the form of the Graduate, grotesquely playing and missing at his first three balls, before suddenly announcing himself to be a born-again right-hander, and smacking the next three into a neighbouring postcode in his traditional, uncomplicated style.

'What happened to the "I was put on earth to be an elegant left-hander" bit?' I asked him.

'The rough outside my off stump,' he replied, without batting an eyelid, pointing at a slightly worn patch. 'If we'd batted first, I would have stayed a lefty all the way. You need to be flexible in this game.'

He and the Beekeeper added forty uncomplicated runs in

a style that pointed to a quick and straightforward victory in about ninety minutes' time, before both were caught on the long on boundary to consecutive deliveries. Having not had a good collapse for at least three weeks, we then contrived to lose five wickets in as many overs for not many more runs, at the end of which period our score stood at 60 or so for seven, with just the ninety to make for victory.

It seemed that the only certainty in town was that Alstonefield Cricket Club would get their unbeaten season after all, as they probably expected and deserved.

But then came the second of the year's extraordinary partnerships, following on from the one between the Young Farmer and the Human Sieve back in May at Milton Abbas. The senior partner was the Young Farmer once again, but his brother-in-arms was the Ginger, who graced a cricket pitch no more than three or four times a year, and rarely batted.

'Aristotle is an utter dick,' he had announced during his A Level revision, but he was unwittingly about to prove the old philosopher's dictum that 'quality is not an act; it's a habit'.

It is never a good idea to umpire when one of your children is batting but, by the time the Ginger was out there, my brief innings had flickered gloriously and then died, and I was back in the middle with the white coat on. We don't get many of those days in our lives, but suffice it to say that this was his.

For the first couple of overs, most of the things he hit, either in defence or attack, went in the air into vacant space, and not to hand. Then the short straight boundaries played into his main strength, the lofted drive, whilst the Young Farmer steadily accumulated runs at the other end.

With three overs to go and about twenty runs needed, they brought back the opening bowler. I had deliberately sited myself at the end that he hadn't been bowling, so that when he came back on, as he was bound to, we wouldn't have the potential awkwardness of working together again. But the skipper thought differently, and put him on at my end.

'How about you tell me if he's out, rather than me appealing?' he said in a resigned way, as I took his cap and sweater. For the first four balls of the over, the batsmen traded quick singles and it wasn't until the fifth that the delivery crashed into the Ginger's front pad. Ten people on the ground shouted their appeal, but the bowler announced for himself that it wasn't out because it was going down leg, which it was.

If he hadn't, I would probably have given it.

On they went in their contrasting styles until, with three runs needed, the Ginger latched on to a short ball on his leg stump and speared it to the square-like boundary for the victory. Whereas our win against West Heath had come from a squeaky mis-hit off the final ball, this was, by our own standards, both competent and relatively calm.

We walked off the ground in the low September evening sun – batsmen, fielders and umpires – bottling deep within ourselves that near magical feeling of a close game played between mates in a beautiful place. A few weeks later, Alstonefield's match report showed that the defeat had hurt them a great deal, as the club had never got through a season before undefeated, but there and then they were too polite to show it.

Back at the George Inn, among the heavy oak garden tables and flitting bats, we toasted the dying season to the background noise of the Gun Runner and Ahmadullah still banging on about pomegranates.

11 The Finer Points of Nudity

October

I was at Gatwick, having an Ely.[1]

September had gone, and with it all memories of the drought, the unbroken weather, and the unexpected luxury of knowing that, for a time, it would be summer all day, every day. Twelve of us were booked on the Friday morning easyJet flight to Toulouse for our tour of the Dordogne, and the staff at check-in didn't

---

1 From Douglas Adams, *The Meaning of Liff*: 'The first, tiniest inkling you get that something, somewhere, has gone terribly wrong.'

seem to think that the Graduate and I were two of them.

'Look. I shouldn't show it to you, sir, but here is the manifest,' said the irritatingly polite man behind the desk. 'I just can't see your names anywhere. Show me yourself.'

I looked at it, but couldn't. I searched out every possible permutation of my name and looked for its alphabetical start point. Nothing.

'Show me your booking confirmation,' he said, trying to be helpful, but coming over as unpleasantly passive-aggressive. I showed him the email on my phone, and he immediately saw the incriminating evidence.

'Just one problem, sir. Your flight was yesterday. So was his.' I got the impression that telling me this must have been better than sex for him. He had the officious air of someone who had been put on this earth to tell people that they had messed up.

And so, by degrees, my part in the whole wonderful plan faded from sight: the hired minibus, the cheerful fifty-mile drive, the agreeable lunch in the little bistro in Puy-l'Évêque, the swim, the boules, the crossword on the terrace with the first *vin rosé* of the tour. The whole precious order of my long weekend had gone up in smoke, and I hadn't even started trying to buy another pair of tickets, let alone paid for them.

The kind of mess I was in was what happened when people of my age got clever in a digital world, and it explained why my flight had been so much cheaper than everyone else's. My lack of attention to detail had turned round and taken a gigantic bite out of my backside.

I knew how bad it was when all our teammates headed up the escalator to Departures rather than mock us, and smiled thin empowering smiles at us, rather like the yoga women had done all those months before. I could have wept, and probably should have, but there was a high-achieving and exclusive London family huffing their importance behind us in the queue, and I didn't want to give them the pleasure. Right now, all I wanted was to be on my own, swear violently, and then start the process of trying to sort my own mess out.

'Call me when you know what your plans are,' shouted the Tree Hugger, as he disappeared into the level above.

So now I was at Gatwick, having a Wembley.[2]

'YOU and I will open today,' said the Tree Hugger, with exaggerated formality the following morning. We were sitting on the terrace, texting final arrangements to the skippers of the two teams we were due to play in the next couple of days.

'After all, you don't play your first Test match every day.'

With an amount of money that I was embarrassed to admit to anyone, let alone my teammates, I had eventually managed to book us onto another flight later the previous day, and we had made our gradual way from the airport to the house we were staying in.

To profitably fill the five hours between flights, the Graduate and I had taken the train to Brighton, where we sat on the shingle by the pier, throwing pebbles out to sea and at discarded beer cans; then going through every single arcade game, until we had collected enough reward tokens to have earned that most essential of cricket tour accessories, the Pink Princess LED Flashing Head Crown.

---

2 From Douglas Adams, *The Meaning of Liff*: 'The hideous moment of confirmation that the disaster presaged in the Ely (q.v.) has actually struck.'

Our arrival during dinner had, of course, prompted the pent-up barrage of ridicule from the others; ridicule that I not only expected, but would have felt robbed not to have received.

There are eight functioning cricket teams in south-west France, populated not so much by the locals, but by expats who have either moved out there to work, or have traded in a life of toil and obscene house prices in England for one of indolence and value down there. The local *mairies* are happy enough to give them basic facilities, as they themselves are subsidised by the state for each different sport they can come up with.

The downside is that the teams have to operate on basic matting wickets embedded on concrete blocks, and in the middle of an outfield that is anywhere between dodgy and lethal on which to field. The pavilion arises on match day in the form of a canvas lean-to, and the changing rooms are situated behind a tree somewhere, to the left of an old cement mixer with a wheel missing, hard by the *bricolage* of unused building materials.

The nearer you get to Toulouse, as a rule, the more likely you are to encounter Airbus employees from all over the world, dripping in first-class degrees from prestigious universities and colleges, and with sports qualifications to match. The first time we went to France, where we had expected Jean, we got instead Jamal, and he had proceeded to teach us a strong lesson in the dangers of traditional national stereotyping.

For in the last thirty years or so, the diaspora of cricket players from the Commonwealth has started a fire of enthusiasm wherever it has gone, which the British have never even begun to manage. Once we had lost the empire, it was as if we decided that there were enough people playing cricket already in the world, and to involve more risked only establishing a wider pool of countries who could then beat us. Nowadays, over eighty per cent of the French national team have their origins on the Indian sub–continent.

Overseas tours change the dynamics of a club more rooted, as they tend to be, in adventure and hedonism, and less in routine and excellence. Over the years, a few basic rules have emerged.

Ten golden rules for cricket tours in France

1. Everyone always says that they will come when the tour is first announced. They do this because they want to leave the door open until the last possible moment, in case they find a way of being allowed to go. In fact, no one is in the team until they have emailed the receipt for their booked flight.

2. If you find yourself wondering for more than five seconds if someone will fit in, they won't.

3. Inevitably, someone will think that a pint in Wetherspoons at 5.45 a.m. is a good thing, not because they remotely want one, but because they think mythology will expect them to have had one. Wetherspoons airport pubs are consequently full of quarter-finished pints.

4. Touring virgins must make a contribution of a bottle of Monkey Shoulder triple malt Scotch whisky. That is their buy-in.

5. The Wealth Manager always starts a food arms race in any given restaurant, meaning that eleven budget tomato salads suddenly metamorphose into eleven steak tournedos in a

rapid and financially suicidal exercise in mutually assured destruction.

6. The kitty has never got enough money in it. Until the last day, when it always has too much. Hence, the treasurer never really enjoys the tour.

7. The designated driver is provided with free drinks for his sacrifice, which is a shame, as the law prevents him from ever taking advantage of this.

8. The locals really couldn't care less about what you are doing. They would be more interested in a lecture on dialectical materialism than in learning not to move behind the bowler's arm. They are beyond help.

9. Like the first cuckoo of spring, what players really think of other players only ever emerges on the final night of a given tour, once the Monkey Shoulder has gone.

10. Whatever they say before the tour, no one *actually* wishes to visit that historic castle, those caves or that nice museum, on the Saturday and Sunday morning. They want to go to a vineyard. Any vineyard. And they want to stay there as long as possible.

On the Saturday, we were playing our first ever international, against Andorra, a team set up a few years before so that a Dutch touring side had someone to play against. Because they are on their own in that little country, the one prerequisite for an Andorran cricketer is to enjoy long car journeys, and they were making an eight-hour round trip for this encounter, on a ground that we had borrowed for the occasion at Damazan, just south of Bergerac.

The issue with travelling deep into another country for a cricket match is that it can quickly become a retrospective exercise in the management of expectations. It is one thing to drop a sitter twenty miles from home, and to be carted for fourteen runs off the only over you bowl, but quite another to do it six hundred miles away, and having drained the housekeeping budget to make the trip. So, after losing the toss and being put in to bat, the Tree Hugger and I found ourselves walking out to the middle with varying degrees of apprehension.

Ahead of us as we walked were the blue hills of Bergerac, and to our right was a half-harvested field of sunflowers on a slight rise; but it was the campsite and adjacent nudist colony on our left that drew most of our attention, with its perplexing sight nearby of a tubby, middle-aged Frenchman abandoning his skimpy speedos to let it all hang out, and of his other half cupping her own breasts appreciatively in the sunshine. This was not a view that our sport normally afforded us, and we weren't entirely sure what to do with it.

In the event, it took no more than two balls to continue the theme of my weekend.

The first one, quick and bowled on a good length, struck a lump in the concrete below the matting and suddenly reared up to strike me full on the chest. Professional sportsmen are trained not to show hurt, but I was no professional, and, anyway, the force of it had half knocked me off my feet. The Tree Hugger, the bowler and the wicket-keeper all stood around me making sure I was alright, whilst I gingerly fingered the bruising on my chest, where the seam mark of the brand-new ball had implanted its pattern into my skin.

'Take a break,' advised the Tree Hugger, 'and then come back out when you're ready.'

But of the two available versions of me, the sensible one was already off the pitch and visiting some local vineyard and discussing the coming *vendage* with the grower, and it was left to the idiot 'I want to be a hero' one to deal with the current situation.

'I'm fine,' I lied, and so the wicket-keeper duly put his gloves back on, the bowler went to the top of his mark, and the Tree Hugger to his own batting crease at the other end.

In truth, my body was fine, bar the bruising, but my mind definitely wasn't. Many things went through it as the bowler ran up to deliver his next ball: attack, defence, aggression, respect, going forward, staying back, and, for all I know, probably even the nude lady a hundred yards to our south.

But principally what went through my mind was self-preservation. If it had happened once, it could happen again, and, fatally, I held my bat up vertically in front of me to protect my chest from the straight ball coming towards me. The ball didn't rise, moved slightly off the seam, kissed the bottom edge of the bat, and went through to the keeper.

I looked at the umpire, possibly in some crazed expectation that he would articulate sympathy with my predicament and call me back on the basis of some fictional no-ball. Then I tucked the bat under my arm and walked slowly back to the tent on the boundary, reflecting on the two air tickets, hundreds of pounds and two days of effort it had taken to achieve my two-ball international duck.

'How did that go?' asked the Beekeeper, who had been getting something out of the minibus during the entire length of my little innings.

For the next hour, it was partly about the growing group of nudists who had joined the tubby Frenchman and his wife for their al fresco picnic, but mostly about the Tree Hugger.

'Every dog has its day,' remarked the Sieve cheerfully, as the Tree Hugger fended off a couple of rising deliveries from his chin. 'And maybe this is his.'

Like most clichés, this one struggles to be sustained for any length of time, but it was beginning to look possible that the Tree Hugger might actually be having that mythical day himself.

He had not enjoyed the best of seasons and, like me, he didn't really expect to these days. But he also had a deep love for the game, and a corresponding personal need to amount to more than simply being the bloke who organises matches for other people. However, unlike me, he didn't have a family to go back home and take it out on, or dogs to kick, after a bad game. So he would just head back to his empty house and watch disappointment bouncing off the sitting-room walls. As a result of all this, when the Tree Hugger failed early in an innings, he always needed time on his own before he reintegrated himself with the others.

But at Damazan, after the scratchiest of starts, he began ball by ball to get on top of the bowlers, starting with a couple of lusty, lofted blows down the ground. Slowly he grew in confidence; sometimes deep in defence if a good bowler was on, or we had lost a wicket, sometimes in bold attack when they weren't, or when he had got confused. When he got to thirty, I went out to umpire, so as to be in the action, but also to keep him fed between the overs with vapid advice, and with some old Starbursts from a previous season that I had found in a pocket of my cricket bag.

The remainder of the White Hunters seemed to be less and less focused on the cricket, though, and more and more focused on Monsieur and Madame Tubby and their friends in the nudist club. One by one, they found excuses for why they needed to be at the other end of the ground from the makeshift pavilion;

staring over the low hedge into the compound as, one by one, the nudist picnic became better attended and worse clothed. The Gun Runner produced a couple of off-colour, *Franglais* remarks, which made the rest of us wince, but made him as happy as he had been all day.

But through all of it, the Tree Hugger ploughed on, mixing up his approach, occasionally getting lucky as balls fell to earth in vacant areas of the ground, and once when he should have been run out by a mile, but wasn't. As one of his best friends, I knew and loved so much of what he was experiencing as he passed through the thirties and forties, but a tiny bit of me was wishing that it could have been me. A sliced four over point brought him to his fifty, and he duly raised his bat and trotted into the pavilion as an honourable retiree.

We waited for the Sieve to come up with another socially apposite cliché, but he was too busy padding up, and practising his offside wafts.

Out in the middle, the Graduate and the Young Farmer started to take an awful toll of the Andorran attack, which had lately become less of attack and more of an apology, adding fifty runs each, and enabling us to complete our thirty-five overs at 230 for six. We watched them walk in, all smiles and casual glove pumping, and we knew in our hearts that the difference between us and them was that they knew they could go on doing this for decades to come, and we knew deep down we couldn't.

Pushing the age of sixty from one side or the other, as the Tree Hugger and I were, we couldn't exactly hear the clock ticking, but we knew it was out there somewhere beyond the horizon. Of all the things you lose in the ageing process, it is the sense of immortality that is the hardest. But of all the things you gain, the most comforting is the sense of value that you get from the here and now – unless you count the taste for expensive wine.

WE went out to field with a spring in our steps, and the Tree Hugger placed each fielder with the pedantic precision of a ballet choreographer. I shuffled off to a place I felt was a good compromise between where he had asked me to go, and where I actually wanted to be. That's how it's supposed to work: the captain's placements are for the guidance of wise men and the strict adherence of fools.

'No,' he said testily. 'I want you at point. Go out ten. No! Another five. OK? Thank you.'

I wanted to tell him that I wasn't a child, but equally, I wanted to leave room for me to behave like one if I felt like it later in the afternoon, and so let it pass.

The Breeder lumbered up to bowl the opening ball of Andorra's innings. It was a long hop outside the off stump, and their opening bat cut it sumptuously towards exactly where I had been placed.

'One run!' shouted the batsman.

'Keeper's end,' shouted the Graduate urgently, waiting for me to collect the ball and drill it back in with a careless flick of the wrists. All the shouting made me look up, and in the act of looking up, the ball bounced over my outstretched hands and continued on its merry way down towards the boundary and the nudists beyond.

There is something very personal about a bad misfield, like an ill-advised joke told in a room that has suddenly gone silent, or an embarrassingly isolated political opinion. But the general view at this stage of the afternoon was a forgiving one, and, so long as it didn't become a regular occurrence, all would be well.

'Sorry,' I said to the Breeder, once I had trotted off to the boundary to retrieve it, who replied that it was no problem and duly went back to his mark to prepare to deliver the second ball. I clapped my hands vigorously as he ran in, so as to denote both enthusiasm and alertness. When he delivered it, the batsman cut it sumptuously enough in my direction again, but this time straight to me on the full.

'Catch it!' suggested the Young Farmer.

This is a curious habit that has only developed in the last few years, whereby younger members of the team, obviously worrying that the older players won't have noticed the ball in the air coming in their direction, or perhaps wouldn't know the rule about catching, see fit to articulate it.

Normally I take most of the catches that I am offered, but this wasn't a day for normal. It was coming fast at waist height, an easy reflex catch, but I snatched at it, catching only the ends of my fingers as it sped its way to the nudists. The batsman did some gardening in his crease by way of indicating that it had all been deliberate, and that he intended to stay there a long time. I wrung the guilty pain from my fingers, and headed back out to the boundary to retrieve the ball.

'Sorry,' I repeated to the Breeder, who assured me slightly sadly that it was of but little consequence, and could have happened to anyone. Eight for no wicket off two balls.

As the game wore on, I found myself being moved to ever more inconsequential places in the field, until I ended up amongst the anonymity of the sunflowers and sawdust at fine leg. Wherever I went, the ball chased me, and whenever it chased me, I managed to mess up the simple act of getting it back to the Sieve behind the stumps. Eventually, I knew that the team had collectively arrived at the unspoken conclusion that one of their players was bringing the roof down on them, a sentiment conveyed with understated British elegance by the body language. Only the Sieve seemed not to care, possibly because he drank from the same well of incompetence.

'Ooops,' he said, as another shot sped between my legs.

Thus we failed to protect our enormous total, and thus we watched Andorra romp past it during the early part of the penultimate over. Other people had screwed up as well, to be fair, and the outfield was without question uneven and tricky, but it is human nature to require a scapegoat for each failure it undergoes, and the goat in question had to be me. I was an old goat, and I would have needed a lot of marinading to be a half palatable one, but I was unmistakably a goat. A little bit of me wished that I minded more.

I knew how deep the problem went when the Graduate came alongside me at the presentation and asked if I was alright.

'You know, it doesn't matter, all of this,' he said.

'What doesn't matter?' I was still in the 'I am a miserable sinner' phase of recovery, and I hadn't reached the 'we're all one big, happy, supportive family' one yet. The parent-child relationship was temporarily reversed, and he headed off to talk about adult things with the grown-ups, whilst I wandered across the ground to see if I could join in Monsieur Tubby's little picnic. I'd actually enjoyed the game, despite my grand lack of contribution, but I realised that a little bit of absence might help my teammates forget any of my deficiencies.

THE nature of a White Hunter tour is not, contrary to popular belief, tied up in the unfeasible quantities of alcohol that get consumed – with a couple of notable exceptions, we are well beyond anything remotely impressive in that line these days – or even in the sport we play, but in the sense of shared endeavour, and the dynamic, flowing nature of the tour itself. The cast stays more or less the same, but the action moves from place to place so that, in each of them, each player gets a different sense of perspective, and is refreshed by it.

It is all tied up in Heidegger's philosophy of time and space, apparently, whereby people understand themselves as part of the changeable interaction of man and the world. Or it's that we all like a bit of variety in our lives, I forget which.

For a few precious days, the strict stopwatch of routine is turned off, the to-do list abandoned, and a person can go back to doing things at short notice purely because they happen to look quite fun. Either way, it took our minibus an hour and a half more than it should have to get back to our accommodation that evening, due to first the Land Agent, then the Gun Runner, finding watering holes that they felt would have been criminal for us to have driven by. We were no criminals, and so we dropped in each of them to ensure we stayed on the straight and narrow.

Later that night, we invented a new sport. It's what the British have always done.

Keeping our squad of elite athletes at the peak of their capabilities during the tour was not necessarily uppermost in the Tree Hugger's mind, or mine. But, over the years, we had come to realise that men of a certain age are very profitably diverted from overeating and alcohol abuse by the prospect of playing with round balls of almost any size, material or weight, and that this can also lead to enhanced performance.

Once it grew too dark to keep playing table tennis and football, we turned our attention to a beautiful set of boules, a numbingly tedious game in its traditional format, but a life-enhancing one when you introduced darkness, steep hills, undergrowth and a large river 300-foot below into the equation.

In this way, Extreme Pétanque was born, a sport that managed to combine the cultural heritage of the French peasant with the risk factors of, say, scree running, or parascending, and with the ill-disguised violence of a mixed martial arts club thrown in. It was far from the traditional village square game where the *cochonet* (or jack) is dispatched across the *piste* (or green) by the *homme grincheux en beret* (grumpy bloke in a beret); instead the *cochonet* is hurled over into the *sous-bois ci-dessous* (undergrowth far below) by the *jouer de cricket sans espoir* (hopeless cricketer).

Once the *cochonet* has come to a rest, each player has to follow it over the *barriere* (gate) and run through the pitch black, down the near vertical wooded hill, until he has retrieved it; fighting off all comers on his way down. In this pursuit, in a touch of genius arrived at by the Graduate, he is armed solely with an 800-gram, boxwood-and-steel pétanque ball, which he is expected to utilise only when in hand-to-hand contact with an opponent. The winner is the one who is holding the *cochonet* with one hand, whilst attached to the parasol on the terrace with the other.

All of which may help to explain why, as a fighting unit, we were perhaps not at our physical best at 3.00 a.m., as we turned in for the night's sleep that would lead to our third-time-lucky attempt to beat Catus Cricket Club, a few miles down the road.

'I've got a funny feeling about this one,' said the Tree Hugger.

12 Monkey Shoulder

October

THE final day of our season started with a clap of thunder, with the last of an overnight storm rumbling its way out of the valley.

It took me a second or two to work out why my body was even more of a disaster area than normal for this time in the morning, when, for the most part, it had simply been a walk-on extra in yesterday's match. It would have been understandable if I had scored a gritty seventy and bowled seven tidy overs, but I hadn't; I had compiled a gritty nought and had not been allowed anywhere near bowling the ball. Then I remembered the Extreme Pétanque, an activity that, to be honest, had seemed rather cleverer at two in the morning than it did right now.

I texted Caroline to see how things were at home, and she sent back: 'All good, thanks. Off to Tate Modern. Hope you score lots of runs today xx.'

I thought about it for a second. I had the captaincy for the Catus match, and my first delicate task was to choose one of the twelve to sit out the match. I lay in bed, watching the anvil-headed clouds bundling away to soak some other area, and went though the options. Five or six of the players simply contributed too much in terms of cricketing skill to be dropped: we actually wanted to win this match. The remainder were a mixture of people who would either make it ridiculously easy for me to leave them out, or would fight their corner energetically.

I thought of the Tree Hugger and the contribution he had made the previous day. Maybe it should be him. But, as the minutes passed, I knew with increasing certainty that it should be me. Not because I had suddenly become some unassuming Type B saint, nor even because my level of contribution didn't merit kicking anyone else off the team.

No, it was because, for the first time in over thirty years, it seemed a perfectly logical thing to do because I *could* do it, and I didn't really mind. Instead, I would umpire throughout the game, and someone else could captain. That way, my injuries would slowly heal and, besides, it was unlikely that the gesture would go unappreciated among my teammates.

This act of self-sacrifice, significant though it might have been to me, was rendered null and void immediately on my arrival downstairs in the dining-room, which was less a place to eat than a scene from the casualty clearing station at Passchendaele. The Extreme Pétanque had taken a fearful toll on even the younger bodies, but what it had done to the older ones was something else. Cuts, bruises, gashes and sprains were the residual evidence of a group of people who had decided to suspend adulthood for the evening, and were now paying the consequences. As an act of collective self-harm, it was hard to top.

We lacked medical experience as a team, but basic triage established that, while most of us could probably scrape through a game of cricket, the Gun Runner was a non-starter. His ankle was three times the size it should have been and facing in a strange direction. Moreover, it didn't look like a limb that would get better on its own with the passing of time; it needed an X-ray at the very least, probably an operation.

The Land Agent said that he had seen lesser injuries leading to amputation when he had been a soldier, but he was hopeful that the Gun Runner's life could be saved, even if the leg couldn't. We told him all this, as the Tree Hugger was applying a few damp tea towels by way of a compress, and accepted with shame that what we had done last night was not the best preparation for a match we had travelled six hundred miles to play.

After all, we had been beaten by Andorra the day before, a lesser team, whilst we were in prime condition; what Catus might do to us in the state we were in didn't bear thinking about. Various other players came up with suggestions for what we could do to finish off the Gun Runner, until the Tree Hugger told us all to grow up and start taking it seriously.

The Beekeeper suggested we go and reflect on our stupidity at a small bar he had spotted on the Boulevard Léon Gambetta in Cahors. It wouldn't mend the Gun Runner's ankle, he conceded, but it would make the rest of us feel so much more positive about the coming game. In a world that had gradually grown devoid of good plans, this was at least the germination of one, and we agreed that the brasserie Au Bureau Cahors, wittily named so that customers can say they are *au bureau* (in the office), was where we all needed to be.

OF the fifteen top things that TripAdvisor recommends you to do in the small village of Catus, a few miles outside Cahors, cricket isn't one of them.

La Plage aux Ptérosaures beats it by a mile, as does the *Cap Nature* and even the farm machinery museum. In fact, it isn't even the top thing to do in its own four-acre deserted field, trumped as it is by the adjacent *Plan d'Eau*. It probably wouldn't be up there if you extended the list to one thousand things but, nonetheless, Catus has a cricket club, a ground, a team and a pedigree. As with all far-flung sports adventures, Catus CC is the result of years of hard graft by a few die-hard volunteers, and then, in 2007, by an act of stunning generosity by the sports-mad mayor of the village, who made over a patch of land down by the lake, and the money to do something with it.

A glance down the match reports on the club's website shows not only the eclectic mix of cultures and backgrounds that make it all up, but the fact that they are regularly the best, or second-best team in the south-west of France. Bangladeshi, Sri Lankan, English, Australian and even Irish rub shoulders in the alluring melting pot of the Dordogne, and the only thing missing is a French accent.

The first time we had travelled down there, this being our fourth visit, we had completely underestimated the potential strength of their competitiveness, and had fortified ourselves rather too well for the match at some riverside bistro that had caught the Wealth Manager's eye. The matting wicket demanded a different technique than we had in mind, and more patience than all but a couple of players were prepared to demonstrate, and we capitulated in the sunshine.

It was one of those defeats when the opposition captain wonders for a minute or two whether he shouldn't offer a quick, extra beer match to use up the allotted time, but then thinks better of it. We never made those simple mistakes again, but we had run out second against a better team on each of our next two visits. Right up until the shenanigans of the previous night, we had been quietly confident that we had the right infusion of youth and talent to turn the tables around this time.

As the skipper for the day, I made a suitable rallying call to the assembled team on the terrace of Au Bureau Cahors and started with the suggestion that we moderated our intake of alcohol out of respect to our ambition, and to the hospitality of our hosts. The Wealth Manager duly put the *carte des vins* back down on the table with a reflective sigh, the *Château du Cèdre Cahors* a mere fleeting memory in the far-flung reaches of time.

'If I win the toss, I think we will bat first,' I said. 'Keep them out in the field in the heat of the day.'

An hour later, and only after the Breeder had incurred not one, but two traffic-offence fines for the imaginative way that he had tried to traverse Cahors to get to the ground, I had duly lost the toss.

'We'll have a bat, if you don't mind,' said the skipper. I could hardly tell him that, yes, I did mind, and that actually I would prefer them to field. I walked back to where the White Hunters were immodestly climbing into their cricket kit in the nearby undergrowth, and told them the news. We had fashioned a rude pair of crutches for the Gun Runner out of a couple of small fallen branches, and I told him that his punishment was to umpire in the hot sunshine until his leg could take it no more.

He donned a sunhat, lit a reflective Balkan Sobranie cigarette and hobbled his way out into the middle, in a way that would have had Frederick Forsyth licking his pencil in anticipation of the back story.

The Catus batsmen were on the back of a slightly embarrassing collapse against their arch-rivals, Eymet, the previous weekend, and they treated the opening overs from the Graduate and the Young Farmer with perhaps more respect than they merited. Flowing drives and rasping pulls were replaced by the block and the exaggerated leave, a runless shot that still has the Sieve gasping in admiration every time he watches it played.

Whilst we weren't taking any wickets, they weren't scoring many runs and, as their innings was limited to thirty-five overs, that suited us quite well. After a while, and really just to ring the changes and disrupt the batsmen, I called the Young Farmer up from his position at fine leg to leg slip; it was the kind of thing that a captain does only when he wishes to create the illusion of a grand plan, more to impress his own teammates than to boss the opposition.

Setting a leg slip for an indifferent bowler is much like a rookie golfer taking out hole-in-one insurance, or a Russian oligarch buying a Premiership football club in the humorous notion he will eventually make money out of it. But the very next ball, the right-handed opener flicked a shot off his toes that had got slightly quick on him, and put it straight in the path of the diving leg slip, who proceeded to pouch the catch of the season.

'Top catch!' they all said to the Young Farmer, during our self-congratulatory huddle in the middle. 'And top field placing! How did you work that one out?' I said nothing, tried to look deeply astute and wandered back to slip.

The very next ball caught the outside edge of the new player's bat, and flew high up to my right, straight into a hand that happened to be in its way. And not just any hand. My hand.

Salmon-like would be over-egging the quality and speed of the jump, as it was more in the style of a breaching whale; but it was by some distance the best catch I had ever taken on a cricket pitch, and the strangest thing was that I never thought it would do anything other than stick. The skill was now to accept the plaudits as if the whole thing was mere routine.

Even though the fourth wicket pair progressed with ambition, the Bangladeshi with exquisite deftness, and the Irishman with uncomplicated brutality, we never came close to losing the plot. Every time they threatened to break away, we held them back. We toiled away in the sun, snapping up sharp chances where they were offered, stopping hard-driven balls and hurling them in on the pick-up.

Quite how the Hogarthian parody of athleticism that had gathered round the breakfast table six hours ago had metamorphosed into this was unclear, but we had, and that was all that mattered. Quite often, in these circumstances, we are inclined to end up in different grid references to the plot, but occasionally we amount to a proper cricket team, complete with ambition, a plan and, above all, the means to carry it out. It was thrilling to be a part of it. Merely to get your hands on those fleetingly rare moments, when a team of people get to amount to more than the sum of their parts, is to look over the wall into the pleasure garden. Many people go through a lifetime without breathing in its scented glories.

'This is better than sex,' said the Young Farmer, who had traversed half the pitch to come and give me this opinion. 'Just don't let up on them now.'

'What did he just say?' asked the Engineer from behind the stumps. 'Did he say it was better than sex?'

'Something like that.'

'Blimey,' she exclaimed, as everyone took their positions for the new over. 'Doesn't that depend on who with? He needs to get out more.' She looked genuinely shocked.

After some agricultural blows towards the end of their thirty-five overs, Catus posted a respectable 205 for nine. With a relatively even strip, and a lightning-fast outfield, it was one of those totals that slightly flattered the batting side, whilst still leaving their opposition knowing they had to score at about a run a ball. However, the White Hunters' capacity to implode at the drop of a hat was the stuff of legend, so we needed to factor in a plan to take that into account.

As the Tree Hugger had said the previous night: 'I've got a funny feeling about this one.'

They don't do traditional teas in these parts, so we had to settle for Orangina and pastries instead. But if you could bottle moments of your life and preserve them, the tea interval that followed would have been a strong candidate. In a messed-up, high-pressure world, our little group had come together as a result of birth, friendship, shared interest and pure accident, and we were all doing stuff that we loved, with people we loved as well.

Our individual lives may well have been imperfect and complicated, and deep down more than a few of us probably had reason enough to dread going back to work on the Tuesday morning, but for now we were living a short, simple dream, and that was enough. To share a season, even a bit of a season, with this effect is something that is theoretically open to everyone, but the reality is that most people would never even think of trying it.

When social teams die, it is probably most often because they fail to deliver enough of these magical moments to the regular players. Deprived of the target of promotion, or a cup run that holds a league team together, a social or wandering team needs a little bit of success washed down with the consistent feeling of time well-spent.

It's not necessarily the victories, or an aggregation of the individual bits of brilliance, that keeps it all on the road. It's those tiny bankable bits of memory that, when re-minted at some point down the line, remind the players that they were simply happy doing what they did, with the people they were doing it with, and have enough confidence that there will be more to stick around.

THE Tree Hugger and I agreed to alternate the batting order with thumpers and blockers, of which we had about equivalent numbers, and simply hope it came off, but what happened next didn't even feature in our wildest dreams.

Needing a rate of roughly run a ball to win the match, the Tree Hugger (a blocker) saw out the first over without scoring. This, in technical terms, is called 'having a look', and theoretically allows the batsman to see the pace, bounce and carry of the wicket, before committing themselves to more aggressive shots.

The first ball of the second over, the Graduate deposited into the Ruisseau du Vert, a small stream to the north of the pitch. Doing this off your first ball is called, in technical terms, 'taking the piss'. The second ball ended up in the same bit of water, but via a different trajectory and one bounce on the outfield.

Whilst the ball was being retrieved with an old shrimping net, the Tree Hugger met the Graduate for a mid-wicket conference, and without being able to hear a word, all of us on the boundary knew exactly what he would be saying: 'OK. Well done. We're up with the rate, so now get your head down and see out the over.' We also knew exactly what the Graduate would be thinking: get this little tricky conversation out the way and then back to business.

The third ball of the over attracted a violent swish and a miss, after which the Graduate practised a modest forward defensive shot to the ribald amusement of both the crowd and the home team. The fourth ball was in the arc, and was hit with such blistering ferocity that it cleared the stream eighty yards away still on its upward trajectory and ran its way into the car park for the *Plan d'Eau*.

'No one's ever done that before,' said the bowler's wife, who was clearing the tea things with the help of a few White Hunters. 'And we've been here eleven years.'

That left two balls of the opening over, the first of which was scythed over the slip cordon for four, and the last one given an uncomplicated biff for six over square leg. The over had produced twenty-six runs, and the Graduate had played the same 'nine iron' shot to all six of them. Three overs later, we retired him when he got past fifty. The team score was 55, of which the Tree Hugger's share was one.

The Graduate had produced a sixteen-ball half-century by a combination of skill, luck and a mind not to give a damn about whatever happened. It was the first one he had ever scored, anywhere, and it had dramatically reduced the required run rate. Into each sporting life a little sunshine must eventually shine, and this was certainly the high point of his career to date. Perhaps this, I thought to myself, is what happens when you don't submit yourself to yoga, exercises, coaching and psychology.

He grabbed a glass of water, and then came casually over to look at the scorebook, which is what people do when they have exceeded their own expectations. It's a funny old thing, but you don't tend to find someone checking out their score in the book when they've had their stumps flattened third ball.

'Did you see that second six?' he asked me quietly.

The sun was dipping over the tall poplars that ran along the banks of the Ruisseau du Vert as our innings reached its conclusion. For once there were no dramas, for first the Graduate and then the Beekeeper had scored at such a rate that everyone else could simply fill in the gaps around them. The Gun Runner had finally succumbed to the pain in his leg, and retreated to a shady spot on the other side of the ground where he lay fast asleep, with his straw hat covering his face, presumably dreaming of firefights and bullion in the high Iro Mountains of South Sudan.

With twenty-five runs to get, I found myself out in the middle with the Engineer: two players who had contributed the grand total of really not many runs over the season, still less this weekend.

'Didn't think I'd be here doing this at the start of the season,' she said, as she came out to join me in the middle. 'I don't think I've ever played cricket outside Hampshire.' She glanced at the bowler. 'What's he doing, by the way?'

'Not sure,' I said. 'But let's try not to get out to him.'

And we managed. In our rudimentary and varying styles, we chipped away at the target until we were within one lusty blow of it. The shoulders of the Catus players had dropped little by little. Where the ball had been regularly hurled in to the keeper between deliveries an hour ago with meaning and intent, now it was lobbed in underarm by relay; where there had been encouraging shouts of 'on the arm' or 'nice wheels', now there was only faint laughter and the banter of people who knew that cold beers lurked within a cool box on the edge of the pitch. It was a social match, not a league one, and the consequences of the loss for them were no more than transitory.

I finished things with a cover drive all along the ground for four. Those thirteen words cannot begin to convey the rarity of my opportunities to write them down, or even say them. Or how much they meant. Or how much more important to me they were than the fact they had got us over the line to win the match.

At the bottom of the cricketing skills pyramid, among those who love the game, support it and to whom it means an irritating amount, there exists an entire sub-culture of people who dream of executing a cover drive all along the ground for four. The notion of that cover drive for us is a gold standard, like a perfectly risen soufflé for the pastry chef, or an immaculately felled tree for the forester. It is the shot we practise forever with our bats, our umbrellas, our golf clubs, even with a baguette during our French holidays.

Because we don't move our feet like they do in the first-class game, we are fated to wait for that one time when our feet just happen to be in the perfect place for the ball that is approaching. It is what we would ask for in place of our last meal on death row: one more opportunity to produce the shot from heaven.

Once the umpire had signalled the boundary and removed the bails, the Engineer came up to bump gloves.

'Now *that*,' she said, 'just might have been better than sex.'

THE previous season had stuttered to a close with an irritating loss on a damp outfield in Berkshire; this one had skidded into the finishing line sideways, triumphantly, smelling ever so slightly of Monkey Shoulder, out there in the dappled sunlight of a

French field. We had played seventeen matches, won six of them, lost eight and drawn three: where we came from, that outcome was positively Olympian. Personally, my average had scraped into double figures, nowhere near the thirty that I had been aiming for all those months ago, and I had definitively not got a fifty.

When we were back at the house where we were staying, I sat on a low wall at the edge of the terrace for a while and watched Sunday evening rural France going about its business in the valley far below. Tractors pulling trailers full of corn husks and sunflower heads; the first harvesting machines of the *vendage*, positioning themselves for the morning's work to come, when they would start to bring in the *Vin de Pays du Lot*; and the insect-like noise of the passing MBK scooters, each one with its identical cargo of helmetless young men in white T-shirts.

And in-between the scooters and tractors, the fragments of conversations and laughter coming up from the town square, as they played boules and traded gossip, the same as they had been doing for centuries. There was so much that I loved about the way they did things round here, and the pace of life, but ultimately it was destined to be always a holiday love, and six hundred miles to the north was where I belonged. Everything in life was about knowing when to jump out of reality for a while, and when to jump back in again.

'Shower's all yours!' shouted the Beekeeper from the window of our room, and I wandered up to the house to change.

Later that evening, towards the end of dinner, the Sieve started bashing his fork against an empty wine bottle, struggling for the attention of the group; and after a while, he was reluctantly lent their corporate ear.

He looked a bit embarrassed.

'I just wanted to say,' he started, after he had stood up. 'Just wanted to say that stuff like this doesn't just happen. It happens because people make it happen, and they go through all sorts of shit to make sure it happens. Unanswered emails, for example, people dropping out of games at the last minute, oppositions that don't get it.'

He was in the second stage of inebriation, and he dealt with the word 'opposition' much like he had dealt with the leg-stump yorker he had received earlier in the day: with a sudden and ugly stab of effort that thinly disguised the trouble he was having dealing with it.

'So all I really wanted to say to you two,' he leered over at the Tree Hugger and me, conspiratorially, 'was thank you on behalf of us all for all the fun and laughter you bring us. No one else in the northern hemisphere would allow me near a competitive cricket team …'

'They still shouldn't!' shouted the Young Farmer, to general merriment.

'No one else would have given me the chance of playing the game I happen to love, and to come on tour with you all, and be a small part of a great thing. Because I'm that shit. And they're right. So thank you, and please keep it going for years to come. Forever, in fact.'

It might have been funny, but it was also deadly serious, and he was clearly emotional by the time he finished.

He sat down to warm applause, and suddenly I became vaguely conscious that I, too, was holding back tears, albeit different ones. Not many people thank life's organisers, and it was nice that he had, but that wasn't what had suddenly brought me up short. The chill of the autumn night on the starlit terrace high above an oxbow bend of the River Lot gave me the excuse I needed to leave the table and go up to my room to collect a sweater.

Once there, I opened the shutter and looked out, over the

heads of my teammates thirty feet below, across the river and south towards the lights of Bélaye beyond.

'Be a good coach to yourself,' the psychologist had said all those months ago, and, in trying to understand what I was feeling, I felt I was now at least following her guidance, although emphatically not regarding my game. Whilst we still had six hundred miles to travel home, the journey of my season was almost done.

Every one of the four improvements that I had set myself back in the spring had been watered down, or abandoned, during the course of the summer. In consequence, my body was as stiff and sore as it had ever been, and my batting, if anything, was worse. I still believed that every ball I faced would be my last, but, in winning thirty-five per cent of our games, we had at least come accidentally close to one of the targets I had set.

Yoga, hip rotational exercises, technical batsmanship and mindfulness had all been abandoned on the altar of the person I really was, not the person I thought I needed to be. The simple joy was that, by no longer feeling that I needed to be at the centre of the White Hunters' little universe, but could just be a contributor like everyone else, I had quietly shaken off the black dog that trots after false expectation.

I hadn't planned for it to happen, or even noticed it happening; I had just woken up on this day of days and knew instantly that, for whatever reasons, things had changed. Like Pooh and Piglet walking endlessly round that tree in the snow, I had always joined last years' footprints at the beginning of the following season without question: same club, same people, same me. From now on, the footprints could head off to wherever they chose, and I knew deep down that I would cheerfully follow them.

Having started this season wondering if it would be my last, I now knew without doubt that it would all go on forever, and that I would simply be a part of it till one day I wasn't. There are legitimate things to worry about in life, but the unstoppable process of getting a bit older isn't one of them.

I stared back down at the table on the terrace and tried to make out some of the conversations that were going on around the glass-strewn table. It was that stage of an evening when the sense being spoken declines in inverse proportion to its rising volume, and to the heroic number of empties.

At the end immediately below my window, the Breeder was making as cogent an argument as he could to the Tree Hugger about why his traffic infringements were incurred in the interests of the team, and therefore the fines should be met by the kitty, rather than by him personally.

In the middle, the Sieve was cataloguing some of his season's more impressive dropped catches to a group of interested listeners, and how the next season would be so very different, as it always is.

And at the far end of the table, the Gun Runner was talking to the Graduate in a conspiratorial one-on-one. There was too much extraneous noise to pick out more than one in every three or four words, but every now and again I caught a fragment of them on the night breeze:

'Internship … gold … nice bit of South Sudan … three months … bloody good for the CV … what do you think?'

Wondering what Caroline would make of this new development, I closed the shutters, picked up my club sweater and went back down to help them all drain the last of the Monkey Shoulder.

13 Close of Play

THE dying summer does strange things to a cricketer, particularly an antique one. They sense the leaves turning long before the colours change, and they are the first to detect a slight nip in the evening air when they wander out into their gardens. Behind them may be the sun-bleached memories of a heatwave that never relented, and ahead of them the prospect of a long northern winter, but right now all is golden, and it still might never end.

There is a sense that change is coming, but also the uncertainty of not knowing how, and from where. The difference between old cricketers and young ones is that the former can only focus on the season that has just gone, while the latter have magically forgotten it as soon as it is over, and are dreaming of the one to come.

We are lucky as a team that, over the years, youngsters were born and raised to us and, when the sifting had been done, enough of them still liked the game sufficiently to join in and become part of the club.

At first, they often misfired, sometimes misbehaved, but they quickly drew level with and then outstripped the efforts of their fathers. Their gathering strength compensated for our gathering weaknesses. They took what seemed to us suicidally quick singles, bowled long spells, and hurled the ball in from the boundary in ways we had forgotten we could ever do, if indeed we could.

They brought with them an injection of careless *joie de vivre*, because they were young, and because they could still imagine it never ending. They became the reason that we have lasted over thirty years. In the end, they became us, only without the nostalgia.

On my kitchen sideboard lies the club scorebook and embedded within it, the lies it would love to tell, but cannot. If you open it towards the end, it will give you all the runs, wickets and catches, but it won't capture the freshness of a young man leading the team for the first time, or the most human drama behind that most unlikely of victories.

It will tell you of the trip to Staffordshire a few weeks ago; although it will be silent about the Saturday-morning golf at Ashbourne, made nigh impossible by the Friday-evening whiskies at the Hartington Legion. And it will make no mention of us sitting in the garden of the George at Alstonefield, watching bats flit up and down the small road, and hugging the memory of a wonderful match with a team that simply gets it.

Go back a few pages and you will find the bare details of the narrow defeat at Churcher's College that April evening, but it won't describe the one careless flick off the toes that flew for six over square leg, which once again fooled someone into thinking that this season would be different, that this time the runs would flow. But that's all the scorebook does: it provides the statistical architecture for everything else to be hung on, stuck to or absorbed by. For ultimately, all sport is only hope energised or despair postponed.

The end of a season creeps slowly up on you. Then all is quiet.

The kit goes back in the bag, which goes back on the shelf. In eleven houses, eleven small but distinct personal ceremonies take place that lay the season to rest. Make that twenty-two houses and twenty-two kit bags. Make it about three-quarters of a million, because that is the number of active cricketers the ECB came up with in 2015, and they will all be finishing their seasons round about now.

Fewer play this game every year, apparently, and village by village, side by side, it is almost possible to foresee a time, fifty years hence, when it is relegated to the status of morris dancing, milkmen and hay meadows, where bearded men gather together on May bank holidays to keep it going.

A world that compresses entire political philosophies into a Twitter post, or ironic concepts into a single meme, isn't necessarily one that will want to spend six hours on a patch of grass doing not much. Which, paradoxically, is exactly why many of us do it, knowing, as we do, that we live in a world that has forgotten how to be elegantly bored.

It is almost impossible for us to understand why something so life-enrichingly wonderful as this should be declining at all. Most things this good have a waiting list before them, a queue at their start, and a large bill at the finish. Cricket is almost free, and, moreover, it has beer at both ends.

For us, this is our religion, and its glow is always visible out there, somewhere over the treetops. For as long as we are able, the

White Hunter world will keep on turning, and it will continue to offer us its peculiar diet of hope, disappointment and, above all, brotherhood.

Acknowledgements

WHEN you open a crisp, new book for the first time, it is sometimes easy to forget how much has gone into it beyond the author's sweat and tears.

I owe thanks and apologies in equal measure to my fellow White Hunters, whose names are either absent or heavily disguised. Please accept the abuse within as no more than routine, and secretly, I think you may all be rather better than I have allowed you to be. None more so than the Human Sieve, who has defied the process of natural selection for nearly a decade to remain our wicket keeper.

My thanks to Bumble and Louise for giving our club a home, and for welcoming us back season after season with exquisite pitches and wonderful teas. To my sons, Tom and Alex, there goes a special bit of gratitude for allowing the fun to go on long after I feared it might stop, and also to Richard Perkins, for being alongside me on the adventure for a third of a century, so far.

I am very grateful to Andrew Johnston of Quiller for having faith in the first place in my ability to deliver a cricket book that we were all happy with, Ollie Preston for the beautiful illustrations, Dan Norcross for the foreword, and Barry Johnston for editing it with delicacy, assertiveness and occasional bits of sheer genius.

This is among other things the story of a mid-life crisis, and my wife Caroline has been the rock and inspiration for me throughout. I am, as always, primarily grateful to her.

If this book delights and entertains you at all, the credit is heavily theirs.